THE GROUNDED HEART METHOD™

A Parent's Guide to Healing from Within and Raising Emotionally Secure Children

By Justin Sokol

SOKOL PRESS

Published by Sokol Press
www.SokolPress.com

ISBN: 978-1-972295-00-7

The Grounded Heart Method™ and **H.E.A.R.T.-ID**™ are trademarks of Justin Sokol.

To my wife and children,

and to all the legacy-changers.

TABLE OF CONTENTS

Before You Begin — vii

Introduction: The Heart of the Matter — xi

Quick Start: What to Do in a Hot Moment — xvii

How to Use This Book: 5 Steps & H.E.A.R.T.-ID™ — xxi

Chapter 1: Ground the Nervous System — 1

Chapter 2: Reveal the Emotional Root — 37

Chapter 3: Reconnect to the Self — 63

Chapter 4: Lead from a Grounded Heart — 93

Chapter 5: Transform the Family Line — 123

Conclusion: The Journey of a Thousand Repairs — 149

Appendix A: Quick Reference — 162

Appendix B: Troubleshooting Triggers — 163

Appendix C: Tools Index — 166

Appendix D: Online Resources — 167

Appendix E: References & Further Reading — 168

Before You Begin

Disclaimer

The information contained in this book is for educational and informational purposes only and is not intended as a substitute for professional medical advice, diagnosis, or treatment. The strategies and psychological concepts discussed herein—including nervous system regulation and trauma-informed education—should not be used as a replacement for professional therapy or medical care. If any practice in this book increases distress, pause, return to grounding, and seek professional support if needed.

A Note About Case Studies

The case studies in this book are composite educational examples built from common real-world parenting patterns, established research, and widely observed change processes in trauma recovery and nervous system regulation. Names, identifying details, and circumstances have been changed or combined to protect privacy.

These stories are not verbatim accounts of any one person. They are included as teaching tools to help illustrate how **The Grounded Heart Method**™ can be applied in everyday life. While the examples align with principles from attachment science, polyvagal theory, and evidence-informed approaches to trauma recovery, this book is not therapy and is not a substitute for professional care.

My commitment to you is simple: every tool, insight, and example in these pages is grounded in credible psychological research and reflects authentic, accessible pathways for healing through nervous system regulation, emotional awareness, and compassionate self-work.

The Heart of the Matter

When Your Child Becomes Your Mirror

There's a moment every parent knows—the one where your child's behavior triggers something so deep inside you that your reaction surprises even yourself. Maybe it's when your toddler has a meltdown in the grocery store and you feel your chest tighten with shame. Or when your teenager rolls their eyes and suddenly you're transported back to feeling dismissed and small as a child yourself.

In these moments, you're not really responding to your child. You're responding to your own unhealed wounds. I know this intimately, because I've lived it in the moments that mattered most.

This is the heart of the matter: **You cannot consistently give your children the emotional safety you've never received yourself.**

The Grounded Heart Method™ rests on a simple premise: your nervous system shapes your parenting more than your intentions do. Your reactivity is a nervous system issue, not a character flaw. Fortunately, neuroplasticity means you can rewire old patterns. You are not doomed to repeat your past. When you return to safety, your choices widen—and your calm gives your child's nervous system a place to land.

This work requires deep self-examination and may bring up difficult emotions—support is part of the process when you need it. Go at your own pace.

Here's what that looked like for me.

Grounded Heart Story: The Christmas Visit

*I didn't start **The Grounded Heart Method**™ because parenting was going smoothly.*

I started it because I loved my kids, and I could feel how fast my nervous system could hijack the moment—especially when the stakes felt high.

With my son, the stakes have often felt very high. He's far away, and most of our connection has been through FaceTime or the phone. That means our relationship lives inside small windows— sometimes 5 to 15 minutes a week. Our call times are simple on paper: Tuesdays and Thursdays at 4:30 PM his time (EST).

But for a long time, those windows were inconsistent. Missed calls. Late pickups. Attitude. Avoidance. And because I'm working with very little information about his day-to-day life, my mind would fill in the blanks. My system would spike: Do you even care? Am I being ignored?

Here's what changed everything: before our Christmas visit, I decided to stop leading with the grievance.

I didn't ignore the issue. I just chose the order. Regulation first—so connection could follow. I practiced being grounded in front of him: steady tone, open posture, no scoreboard, no 'let me explain why you were wrong.' I focused on being safe. I focused on us.

And something surprising happened.

Since he left, he hasn't missed a single call. Not one. In fact, he's been the one calling me right on time.

That moment became a living case study for me: when I stopped fighting for control and started protecting connection, the problem began solving itself.

From 3,000 miles away, a teenager can easily ignore a reactive parent. But a grounded parent—steady, safe, consistent—can slowly become relevant again, because you stop being another stressor and start becoming a place to breathe.

That's why this work became non-negotiable for me.

Because the goal isn't to "win" a moment. The goal is to become the kind of parent my child can actually hear—near or far. Grounded enough to stay connected. Safe enough to rebuild trust. Clear enough to lead without fear.

*This is the heart of **The Grounded Heart Method**™: regulation first, connection next, guidance last—because behavior follows safety, not pressure.*

What This Book Will Give You

This book will teach you why your child's behavior triggers you, what your triggers are trying to tell you, and how to transform your nervous system into an emotional anchor for your entire family.

You'll learn a five-step healing journey for long-term transformation, and a real-time regulation tool—H.E.A.R.T.-ID™—that you can use in the middle of the hardest parenting moments. Both are explained in full in the next section: *How to Use This Book.*

But before you get to the frameworks, I want you to take one thing with you from this introduction:

Your struggles as a parent are not evidence that something is wrong with you. They are evidence that something inside you is asking to be healed. And that healing is not only possible—it's the most powerful thing you can do for your children.

Let's begin.

If You Only Use One Thing In This Book, Use This...

STEP 0 — SAFETY CHECK (10 seconds)

If you feel out of control, step back. Put space between you and your child. Make sure everyone is physically safe.

STEP 1 — 3-BREATH RESET (20–30 seconds)

Inhale gently through the nose. Exhale a little longer than you inhale (twice if you can). Feel your feet. Name one thing you can see in the room. (This tells your brain: "We're here, now.")

STEP 2 — RUN H.E.A.R.T.-ID™ (60–90 seconds)

Use the Micro-Mantra: "**Name it • Need it • Next it.**"

- **Name it**: What heart-state is here (Protective / Grief / Needs)?
- **Need it**: What's the need underneath (safety, connection, autonomy, worth, competence, rest)?
- **Next it**: What's the tiniest next move that creates safety (regulate, validate, boundary, choice, repair)?

STEP 3 — ONE SCRIPT TO STEAL (10 seconds)

Try this template:

> "I'm here. I see you. We're safe."
>
> "I won't let ______ happen."
>
> "When you're ready, we'll ______."

STEP 4 — REPAIR (later, 30–60 seconds)

If you got loud, shut down, or went too far, repair fast:

"I got overwhelmed and I raised my voice. That wasn't okay. I'm sorry. I'm here now. Let's try again."

If anything in this book feels emotionally intense, go slower. You don't need to "push through." You're building capacity —one safe moment at a time.

The 5 Steps & H.E.A.R.T.-ID™

The Journey and the Tool

This is a practical, tool-based book. Read it straight through, or use it like a guide you return to when real life hits. Either way: one chapter at a time, one small change per week. When you feel activated, flip to *Appendix A* and run the Micro-Mantra: **"Name it • Need it • Next it."** Use the Parent Reflection questions at the end of each chapter to turn insight into a repeatable habit.

Keep it gentle. Progress is measured in faster recovery, clearer boundaries, and more repair—not perfection.

This book is organized around two complementary frameworks:

The 5 Steps are your healing journey—the work you do to change your baseline over weeks and months.

H.E.A.R.T.-ID™ is your real-time regulation tool—what you grab when your nervous system is activated right now.

One builds the foundation. The other gets you through the moment. As you work the 5 Steps, you'll practice **H.E.A.R.T.-ID™** repeatedly—reinforcing the neural pathways that make regulation easier, until what felt conscious becomes more automatic.
The Tool serves the Journey.
The Journey deepens the Tool.

5-STEP JOURNEY & THE H.E.A.R.T.-ID™ TOOL

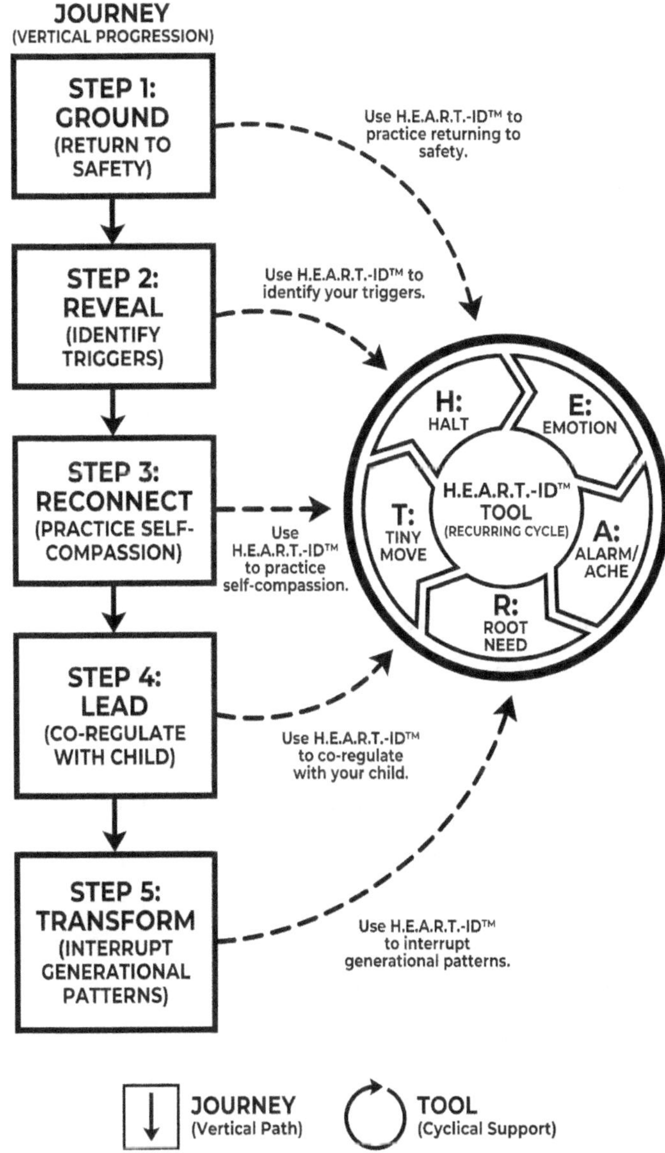

1. Ground the Nervous System

Help the body exit fight/flight/freeze and return to safety.

2. Reveal the Emotional Root

Identify what the trigger is actually about.

3. Reconnect to the Self

Restore trust in your inner voice, emotional truth, and worth.

4. Lead from a Grounded Heart

Integrate new patterns: calm communication, repair, and connection-centered boundaries.

5. Transform the Family Line

Become the emotional anchor so your children inherit emotional safety.

These steps are cumulative. Each builds on the previous. You don't "complete" one and move on—you deepen your practice in all five over time.

And when you need something you can use in the middle of real life—while the baby is crying, while the teenager is yelling, while your body is already flooded—you'll return to the **H.E.A.R.T.-ID™** tool.

H.E.A.R.T.-ID™ | *The Heart Behind the Action*

A trauma-informed micro-skill for parents

Quick Frame: Behavior is the tip. Heart-state is the engine. Core need is the fuel.

Important note: H.E.A.R.T.-ID™ is meant to be used on yourself just as much as on your child. When you run it on you first, you regulate the engine of the moment—so you can guide, teach, and connect from a grounded place.

H — Halt & Ground

Pause. Take a deep breath. Exhale longer than you inhale. Feel your feet. Soften your jaw and shoulders until your body settles even slightly.

E — Emotion Label

Name the emotion and the lane it's in:

- **Protective Hearts (Defense):** Fear, Anger, Shame, Guilt, Control/Hyper-vigilance, Numb/Disconnect

- **Grief Hearts (Vulnerability):** Sadness, Hurt, Loneliness, Overwhelm

- **Needs Hearts (Secure Pursuit):** Connection, Autonomy, Safety, Worth, Competence, Rest

A — Alarm or Ache?

Is your system in **protection** (an alarm/defense response
that wants control, distance, or intensity)? Or is it in **pain**
(an ache/vulnerability response that needs softness,
comfort, or slowing down)?

R — Root/Core Need

Which need is threatened or sought? Choose one or two:

- **Safety**: predictability, protection, calm
- **Connection**: belonging, closeness, attunement
- **Autonomy**: choice, voice, agency
- **Worth**: seen, respected, valued
- **Competence**: capable, learning, mastery
- **Rest**: capacity, play, recovery

T — Tiny Next Move

Choose a small action and script that matches the state:
regulate first, validate what's real, then decide the boundary
or repair.

Scripts that regulate + guide:

- *"This looks like anger. I'm wondering if there's hurt
  underneath."*
- *"Your heart is trying to protect something important."*
- *"I won't let you hurt me or others. I will help you."*
- *"We can be upset and still be respectful. Let's try again."*
- *"I got reactive. I'm sorry. I'm resetting—let's repair."*

H.E.A.R.T.-ID™ (60–90 Second Reset)

> **H — HALT & GROUND**
> Pause. Breathe. Feel your feet.

> **E — EMOTION**
> Name what you're feeling (one word).

> **A — ALARM OR ACHE?**
> Is this protection... or pain?

> **R — ROOT NEED**
> What is this part asking for?

> **T — TINY NEXT MOVE**
> One small, grounded action.

Name it • Need it • Next it

The Micro-Mantra *(the shortcut to remember)*

Name it • Need it • Next it

- **Name it:** "This is anger / fear / hurt."

- **Need it:** "The need underneath is safety / connection / autonomy / worth / competence / rest."

- **Next it:** "My next move is to regulate, validate, and then decide the boundary or repair."

Why This Matters *(brain + nervous system)*

Naming what you feel (a technique Dr. Dan Siegel calls "Name It to Tame It") often reduces overwhelm and brings you back to choice. Research on affect labeling shows that putting feelings into words can quiet the amygdala's alarm response and re-engage the prefrontal cortex—the part of your brain that allows reflection and wise decision-making (Lieberman et al., 2007).

Trauma-Informed Reminders

Children are exquisitely sensitive to adult cues—tone, face, pacing, and volume—and they often match the emotional weather around them. When you regulate first, your calm gives their nervous system a place to land.

- **Safety first:** a regulated adult nervous system leads.

- **All behavior makes sense in context;** we can be curious without excusing harm.

- **Connection and boundaries are not opposites—** both create safety.

- **Repair beats perfection:** *"I got loud. I'm sorry. Let's try again."*

Grounded Heart Story: The Text Message

There's a particular kind of text message that can light up a parent's nervous system like a match.

For me, it's the message that carries an implication—not just information. The kind that makes your stomach drop before you've even finished reading it.

I've experienced this most in co-parenting from across the country. I've had moments where I'm holding my phone, and I can feel my body preparing for a fight... while my mind is still trying to be "reasonable."

This isn't just about co-parenting. It's the same nervous-system spike that can happen with a teacher email, a teenager's tone, or a single sentence from someone you don't fully trust.

One afternoon, I got a message about logistics. On paper, it was simple. In my body, it was not.

My throat tightened. My jaw clenched. My shoulders rose. My fingers were already moving. My breathing got shallow. My thoughts started drafting a response at lightning speed—sharp, defensive, precise.

That's when I caught it:

My body had already decided it wasn't safe.

And that's the whole point: your body gives you clues long before your mind catches up.

So instead of replying, I ran **H.E.A.R.T.-ID™** *on the spot:*

H — Halt & Ground: *feet on the floor, slow exhale*
E — Emotion Label: *anxiety + anger (both)*
A — Alarm or Ache: *alarm — my system wanted control and certainty*
R — Root Need: *safety + respect + clarity*
T — Tiny Next Move: *short, clean, regulated response*

The message I sent was half the length of what my adrenaline wanted to write.

And the best part wasn't whether it "worked" on the other person.

The best part was that it worked in me — it kept me from handing my nervous system the steering wheel.

Now that you've learned the full **H.E.A.R.T.-ID™** framework, you can return to it anytime as your in-the-moment reset. We've provided a condensed cheat sheet of this framework in *Appendix A,* and a link to an interactive online version in *Appendix D.*

Using H.E.A.R.T.-ID™ With Your Child:

While **H.E.A.R.T.-ID™** is primarily a tool for **YOUR regulation**, you can also use it to attune to your **child's heart-state:**

When your child is dysregulated, pause and ask yourself:

> **H** — Can I halt and ground myself first?

> **E** — What emotion are they showing? (*fear, anger, hurt, overwhelm?*)

> **A** — Is this alarm (*protection/control*) or ache (*pain/ vulnerability*)?

> **R** — What need might be underneath? (*safety, connection, autonomy, worth?*)

> **T** — What's my tiny next move? (*validate, offer choice, set boundary, stay close?*)

This keeps you from reacting to the behavior and helps you respond to the heart.

Practice Suggestion:

For the first week, practice **H.E.A.R.T.-ID™** on yourself only. Don't try to use it on your child yet. Just notice your own heart-state throughout the day.

Ask yourself 3 times daily:

- What heart-state am I in right now?
- Is this alarm or ache?
- What do I need?

Once you can reliably identify your own states, you'll naturally begin recognizing them in your child.

Remember:

The 5 Steps are your healing path.

H.E.A.R.T.-ID™ is your real-time reset.

Together, they transform your parenting—not someday, but starting right now, in the next hard moment.

CHAPTER 1

Ground the Nervous System

The Foundation of Everything

The Parent in Fight-or-Flight

Sarah is a devoted mother of two. On paper, she's doing everything right: healthy meals, educational activities, bedtime routines. But when her five-year-old son refuses to put on his shoes in the morning, something inside her snaps. Her heart races. Her jaw clenches. Her voice rises to a volume that surprises even her. "I SAID PUT YOUR SHOES ON! We're going to be late AGAIN!"

Later, after drop-off, Sarah sits in her car feeling gutted. Why did I yell like that? He's just five. What's wrong with me?

Nothing is wrong with Sarah. Her nervous system is doing exactly what it was designed to do: protect her from perceived danger. The problem? Her nervous system learned decades ago that being late meant danger. Maybe her own parents shamed her. Maybe she internalized the message that her worth depended on being perfect, prepared, on time.

Now, when her son moves slowly, her nervous system doesn't register "child being a child." It registers threat.

And when your nervous system perceives threat, it activates one of three survival responses:

Fight

Yelling, controlling, demanding compliance

Flight

Withdrawing, avoiding, shutting down emotionally

Freeze

Dissociating, going numb, feeling paralyzed

These aren't parenting failures. They're **biological survival mechanisms**. But they weren't meant to run the show 24/7.

Sarah came to this work exhausted and ashamed. You met her at the start of this chapter — the mother who yelled about the shoes and sat gutted in the car afterward. But yelling wasn't her only pattern. *"When they start fighting or melting down, I just... freeze,"* she said, staring at her hands. *"I stand there like a statue while they scream, and then I hate myself for it."*

Sarah's nervous system didn't have just one survival mode — it had two. Some days it chose fight: the sharp voice, the volume, the urgency. Other days it chose shutdown: the blank stare, the heaviness, the paralysis. Both were learned early. Growing up with an alcoholic father whose moods were unpredictable, she'd survived by becoming invisible — quiet, compliant, frozen. The yelling came later, after years of motherhood wore down the freeze and something fiercer took its place. Now both patterns were hijacking her parenting, and she couldn't predict which one would show up.

The Breakthrough:

Early on, I introduced Sarah to the Polyvagal Ladder (based on the work of Dr. Stephen Porges). When she saw her "freeze" response mapped onto the nervous system, something shifted. *"So I'm not weak or broken?"* she asked, tears welling. *"My body is just trying to protect me the way it always has?"*

The Practice:

Sarah began using the "**Grounding Through the Senses (5-4-3-2-1)**" technique whenever she felt shutdown coming. Five things she could see. Four she could touch. Three she could hear. Two she could smell. One she could taste. This simple exercise helped her climb back up from dorsal shutdown into ventral engagement—just enough to stay present with her kids.

She also started a daily practice of "Safe Place Anchoring": spending 3 minutes each morning visualizing her back porch (her calm place), noticing the sensations of safety in her body, then placing her hand on her heart and saying, "I am here. I am safe. I can handle this."

The Outcome:

Six weeks later, Sarah reported a profound shift. *"Last Tuesday, both kids were screaming about the iPad, and I felt the freeze starting—that heaviness in my chest, the fog in my brain. But I did the 5-4-3-2-1, and I came back. I got down on their level and said, 'I hear you both. Let's figure this out together.' It wasn't perfect, but I was there."*

The Subconscious "*Background Program*"

Here's what many parents don't realize: in the moments you lose it, you're not failing—you're being run.

Your conscious mind is the part of you that can reflect and choose: I want to stay calm. But your subconscious mind is the part of you that stores what your nervous system learned through experience—especially experiences that felt overwhelming, unsafe, shaming, or unpredictable. It's like a background program designed for survival, not wisdom.

That's why a small moment in the present can create a huge reaction in your body. Your child's defiance, whining, crying, or slow pace isn't just "behavior" to the survival brain—it can feel like a threat to safety, worth, control, or connection.

The Dysregulated Nervous System

Many parents today are living in a chronic state of nervous system activation. Your body never fully lands in safety. Even when things are calm, you're braced for the next crisis: the tantrum, the defiance, the judgment from other parents, the fear that you're failing your children.

This chronic activation

has *Profound*

effects

You misinterpret neutral situations as threatening

(your child's normal developmental behavior feels like a personal attack)

You react from survival mode rather than wisdom

(you yell when you meant to stay calm)

Your body never fully rests

(even sleep doesn't restore you)

Your children absorb your tension

(they become anxious, reactive, or shutdown too)

THE NERVOUS SYSTEM LADDER

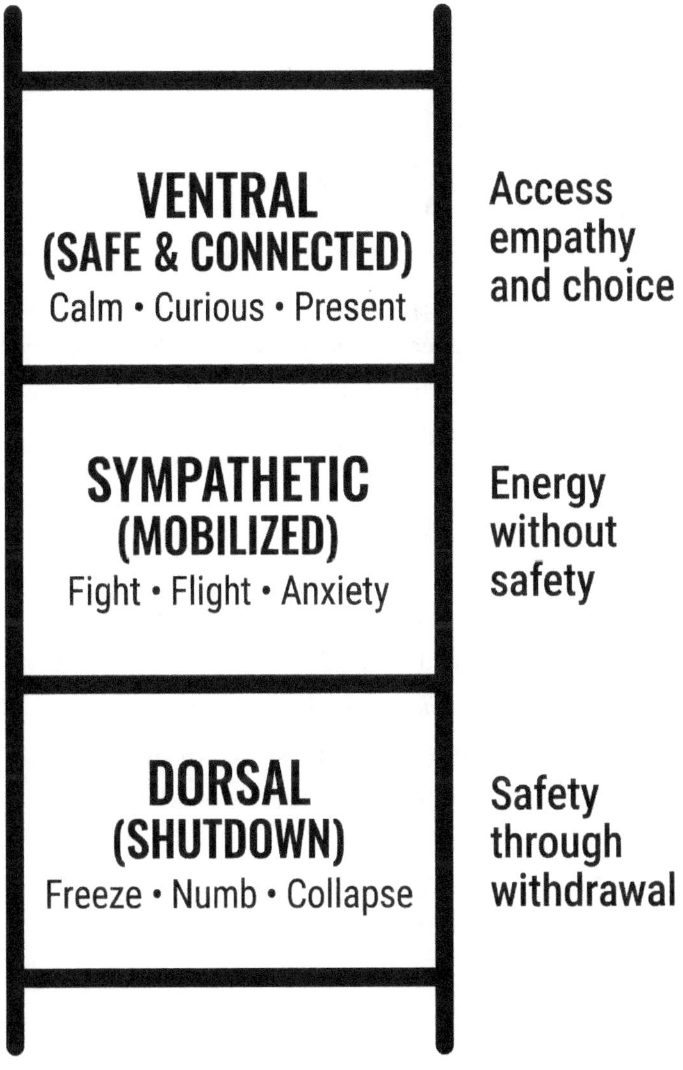

**VENTRAL
(SAFE & CONNECTED)**
Calm • Curious • Present

Access empathy and choice

**SYMPATHETIC
(MOBILIZED)**
Fight • Flight • Anxiety

Energy without safety

**DORSAL
(SHUTDOWN)**
Freeze • Numb • Collapse

Safety through withdrawal

Regulation is about moving one rung
at a time – not jumping to calm.

Marcus arrived for his first session with clenched fists and a tight jaw. "*My wife says if I don't get this anger thing under control, she's leaving,*" he said bluntly. "*I don't want to be this guy, but I can't stop.*"

Marcus's nervous system was stuck in sympathetic overdrive—what he called his "fight mode." Minor inconveniences (traffic, a messy kitchen, his teenage son's attitude) would trigger explosive reactions. He'd yell, slam doors, then feel crushing guilt afterward. "*I sound just like my old man,*" he admitted. "*And I swore I'd never be him.*"

The Turning Point:

When I explained the Polyvagal concept of "sympathetic hijack," Marcus leaned forward. "*You're telling me my body thinks I'm in danger when my kid leaves dishes in the sink?*" He laughed bitterly, but something clicked. His anger wasn't a character flaw—it was a nervous system stuck in threat mode.

The Practice:

Marcus committed to two daily regulation practices:

Morning *"Physiological Sigh"*: Three rounds of double-inhale (through nose) followed by long exhale (through mouth). This well-studied breathing pattern activates the vagus nerve and shifts the system from sympathetic to parasympathetic. Marcus did this in his truck before going into work each morning.

Evening *"Anger Tracking"*: He kept a pocket notebook and rated his anger level (1-10) three times daily, along with what triggered it and where he felt it in his body. This mindfulness practice helped him spot the early warning signs—tight shoulders, hot chest, racing thoughts—before full explosion.

The Tools in Action:

Two months in, Marcus experienced a breakthrough moment. His son forgot to take out the trash again—historically a guaranteed explosion. Marcus felt the familiar surge: heart pounding, fists clenching, rage rising. But this time, he recognized it. He stepped outside, did five rounds of the physiological sigh, and felt his system downshift. When he went back inside, he said calmly, *"Hey buddy, trash needs to go out. Let's take care of it now."*

His son looked shocked. His wife cried with relief.

Your child's nervous system is constantly scanning yours for safety cues.

When you're in fight-or-flight, they feel it—even if you're trying to hide it. Your tension becomes their tension. Your fear becomes their anxiety.

This is why calming techniques that only address the child's behavior don't work long-term. You can't regulate a child from a dysregulated state. It's like trying to teach someone to swim while you're drowning.

The transformation begins when you help your own nervous system return to safety.

THE NERVOUS SYSTEM CONNECTION: CO-REGULATION & SAFETY CUES

WHEN YOU ARE DYSREGULATED (FIGHT-OR-FLIGHT)

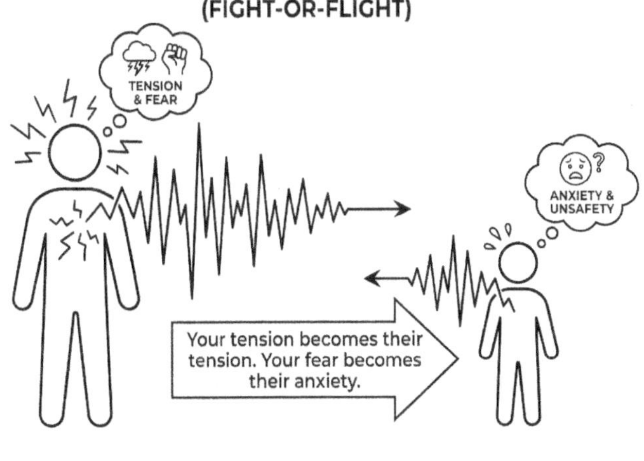

THE 'DROWNING' ANALOGY: YOU CAN'T REGULATE FROM DYSREGULATION

THE STRUGGLE

Trying to teach swimming while drowning.

THE GOAL: REGULATION STARTS WITH YOU

Your calm becomes their safety. Regulation is a shared state.

Calming techniques only address behavior.
True regulation requires your calm nervous system as the anchor.

Keisha described her anxiety as "a smoke alarm that never turns off." Even during calm moments—reading on her couch, watching TV with her partner—her heart would race, her mind would spin with worst-case scenarios, and her body felt wired.

"I've tried everything," she said. *"Meditation apps, breathing exercises, positive thinking. Nothing works."*

The Insight:

When I introduced Keisha to the concept of a chronically activated sympathetic nervous system, she finally had language for her experience. Her body wasn't broken—it was stuck in a state of mobilization that had become her new normal.

The Practice:

Instead of trying to "calm down" (which felt impossible), Keisha began using bilateral tapping: alternating taps on her knees or shoulders while taking slow breaths. This cross-lateral movement helps integrate the brain's hemispheres and signals safety to the nervous system.

She also started a daily "co-regulation" practice with her partner: five minutes of sitting back-to-back, syncing their breath, feeling the support of another regulated nervous system.

The Result:

Within four weeks, Keisha's baseline anxiety dropped noticeably. *"I still get anxious,"* she said, *"but now I have tools to help my body remember it's safe."*

What Does "Grounded" Actually Mean?

In the context of **The Grounded Heart Method**™, "grounded" doesn't mean suppressing your emotions or becoming a robot parent who never feels triggered. It means: Your nervous system recognizes that you are safe, even when things are difficult.

When you're grounded:

You can feel your emotions without being overtaken by them

You can notice your triggers without automatically reacting

You have access to your prefrontal cortex—the part of your brain responsible for empathy, perspective, and wise decision-making

You can stay present with your child even when they're dysregulated

The Window of Tolerance

Imagine your nervous system has a "window of tolerance"—a term coined by Dr. Dan Siegel to describe the zone where we can stay regulated, flexible, and connected.

When you're inside your window of tolerance:

- You can think clearly
- You feel emotionally available
- You respond with patience and empathy
- You can repair after mistakes

When you're outside your window of tolerance (either *hyperaroused* or *hypoaroused*):

- You react impulsively (*yelling, controlling*)
- You shut down emotionally (*withdrawing, numbing*)
- You lose access to compassion for yourself and your children
- Everything feels overwhelming

Traffic Light Check-In:

Here's A simple way to track your nervous system state:

Green — means you're **regulated** and **calm**.

Yellow — means you're **activated**—tension is building but you can still catch yourself.

Red — means you're **dysregulated** and need to step back and ground first.

THE WINDOW OF TOLERANCE

Coined by Dr. Dan Siegel: The zone where we can stay regulated, flexible, and connected.

HYPERAROUSED
(OUTSIDE THE WINDOW: FIGHT/FLIGHT)

❌ You react impulsively (yelling, controlling)

❌ Everything feels overwhelming

RETURN TO REGULATION   RETURN TO REGULATION

INSIDE YOUR WINDOW OF TOLERANCE
(REGULATED & CONNECTED)

✓ You can think clearly
✓ You feel emotionally available
✓ You respond with patience and empathy
✓ You can repair after mistakes

RETURN TO REGULATION   RETURN TO REGULATION

HYPOAROUSED
(OUTSIDE THE WINDOW: FREEZE/SHUTDOWN)

❌ You shut down emotionally (withdrawing, numbing)

❌ You lose access to compassion for yourself and your children

The goal is to notice when you're outside and use tools to return to your window.

Tom came to this work because his adult daughter told him, *"Dad, I love you, but I don't feel like I really know you."* He was baffled. *"I've always been there for her. I worked hard, paid for college, showed up to her games. What more does she want?"*

What she wanted was emotional presence—something Tom had never learned to offer. Raised by emotionally distant parents who valued stoicism and self-reliance, Tom had learned to shut down his feelings and "power through." Now, at 51, he realized this strategy had cost him his marriage and was damaging his relationship with his daughter.

The Discovery:

Tom initially resisted the idea that his nervous system was in "shutdown." *"I'm not depressed,"* he insisted. *"I'm just... practical."* But when we explored dorsal vagal collapse—the kind that doesn't look like sadness but like numbness, disconnection, and going through the motions—he went quiet. *"That's me,"* he finally said.

The Practice:

Tom began with small, embodied practices:

Daily "Body Scan for Aliveness": Lying down for 3 minutes each morning, noticing where he felt numb versus where he felt sensation. This helped him recognize how disconnected he'd become from his own body.

"Reach Out and Touch": Literally placing his hand on objects—his coffee mug, his steering wheel, his dog's fur—and naming the texture and temperature aloud. This practice brought him out of his head and into present-moment sensation.

The Shift:

Three months in, Tom had dinner with his daughter. When she shared a struggle she was facing, instead of offering solutions (his default), he paused, put his hand on his chest (a grounding anchor he'd practiced), and said, *"That sounds really hard. Tell me more."*

She stared at him, then smiled. *"Thanks, Dad. That's what I needed."*

Grounded Heart Story: The Cereal on the Floor

*There's a morning I still think about because nothing "big"
happened—and that's exactly why it matters.*

*It was one of those mornings where the house is already loud
before your brain is fully online. I'd been up late the night before,
and my nervous system was running on fumes. We were already
running late and my daughter was asking rapid-fire questions,
and I could feel my chest tightening with that familiar, quiet
pressure:*

Hurry.
Control this.
Get everyone moving.

*Then the cereal hit the floor. A full bowl—milk, flakes, all of it—
right in the middle of the kitchen.*

*I remember standing there, staring at it, and realizing my body
had gone cold.*

Not angry. Not sad. Just... blank.

*Like someone pulled the plug. My jaw was clenched, my shoulders
were up, and I couldn't find a single helpful word.*

*My wife looked over at me, and I could tell she was waiting to see
which version of me was about to show up.*

That moment was my wake-up call.

I wasn't reacting to cereal.

I was reacting to the internal alarm that says: If things get messy, you're failing.

And when that alarm goes off, my system doesn't automatically choose patience—it chooses whatever kept me safe in the past.

*That's why I built **The Grounded Heart Method**™.*

Because I needed something I could use in real time—not when the house is quiet, not after the kids are asleep, but right there in the spill... when the thinking brain is offline and the body is in charge.

And once you understand that, you stop asking, "What's wrong with me?" and you start asking a better question: "What's happening in my nervous system—and what does it need right now?"

Jennifer sat across from me, hands twisting in her lap, and said, "*I cry at everything. Commercials. My daughter's school concert. Even happy moments. I feel like I'm drowning in feelings, and I hate it.*"

Jennifer was experiencing what neuroscience calls emotional flooding—a state where the intensity of emotions overwhelms the nervous system's capacity to process them. For Jennifer, this wasn't new. She'd grown up in a household where feelings were "too much"—her mother was critical, her father was checked out, and Jennifer learned early to suppress her emotions to keep the peace.

But suppression has a cost. By midlife, all those unfelt feelings were erupting like a geyser, and Jennifer felt out of control.

The Turning Point:

I introduced Jennifer to Dr. Dan Siegel's concept of the "Window of Tolerance"—the zone where we can process emotions without becoming overwhelmed (hyperarousal) or shutting down (hypoarousal). Jennifer's window had become very narrow. Even mildly emotional moments pushed her outside it.

"So there's a reason this keeps happening?" she asked, crying again. "*No*," I said. "*Your nervous system just needs to learn that feelings are safe.*"

The Practice - Month 1:

Jennifer started by labeling the emotion—what Dr. Dan Siegel calls '**Name it to Tame it.**'

When she felt emotions rising, she would pause and say aloud (or write down):

I'm feeling _____ (emotion word). **This feeling is here because** _____ (situation). **My body feels** _____ (physical sensations).

Example: "I'm feeling overwhelmed. This feeling is here because I got an email from my son's teacher about his behavior. My body feels tight in my chest and shaky in my hands."

This simple practice activates the prefrontal cortex (the brain's "observer"), which helps regulate the emotional intensity of the limbic system. Naming the emotion literally reduces its power.

The Practice - Month 2:

Once Jennifer could name her emotions without being
swept away, we added "Emotion Tracking." She used
feelings wheel to identify nuanced emotions (not just "sad"
or "mad," but "disappointed," "resentful," "tender," "lonely")
and rated their intensity (1-10) three times daily.

This practice did two things:
- It helped her see patterns (e.g., she felt most flooded on
  Sunday evenings when anticipating the work week).
- It widened her emotional vocabulary, which gave her
  more precision and control.

The Practice - Month 3:

Jennifer was ready for "Self-Compassion Reframe," based
on Dr. Kristin Neff's work. When big emotions arose,
instead of criticizing herself ("Stop crying, you're being
ridiculous"), she practiced saying:

"This is a moment of suffering."
(Mindfulness - acknowledging the pain)

"Suffering is part of being human."
(Common humanity - you're not alone)

"May I be kind to myself right now."
(Self-kindness - offering care instead of criticism)

She'd place her hand on her heart while saying these phrases, adding a somatic anchor to the practice.

The Breakthrough:

Four months into coaching, Jennifer's daughter had a meltdown about a friendship conflict at school. Historically, this would have triggered Jennifer's own flood of emotions (anxiety, helplessness, maybe even anger). But this time, Jennifer noticed the feelings rising, named them silently ("I'm feeling scared for her and powerless"), took a slow breath, and said to herself, "This is hard. I'm doing my best."

Then she sat down next to her daughter, put an arm around her, and just listened. No fixing. No flooding. Just presence.

Afterward, her daughter said, "Thanks, Mom. That helped."

Grounding your nervous system isn't about meditating for an hour or escaping to a spa (though those are nice). It's about micro-practices you can do in real-time, in the middle of parenting chaos.

Practice 1: The 3-Breath Reset

When you notice activation (*tight chest, racing thoughts, clenched jaw*):

- **Pause whatever you're doing**
- **Place one hand on your heart, one on your belly**
- **Take three slow, deep breaths—inhaling for 4 counts, exhaling for 6**
- **Notice: "*My body is safe right now.*"**

Practice 2: Body Scan Check-In

Several times a day, pause and ask:

- **Where am I holding tension?** (*Jaw? Shoulders? Stomach?*)
- **What does my breath feel like?** (*Shallow? Held? Deep?*)
- **Am I in my body or disconnected from it?**

Just noticing—without judgment—begins to shift your nervous system.

Practice 3:
Grounding Through the Senses (5-4-3-2-1)

When you're spiraling into fight-or-flight:

- **See (5)**: Name 5 things you can see (start with your hands)
- **Touch (4)**: Name 4 things you can feel (start with the ground under your feet)
- **Hear (3)**: Notice 3 sounds in your environment (start with the sound of your own breath)
- **Smell (2)**: Name 2 things you can smell (start with the air)
- **Taste (1)**: Notice 1 thing you can taste

Advanced Nervous System Hacks

Sometimes "just breathing" isn't enough. When you are deeply triggered, you may need to physically stimulate the vagus nerve (your body's "chill out" switch) to get back to the Green Zone.

1. Cold Exposure (The Reset Button)

Cold water on your face triggers the "mammalian dive reflex," which instantly lowers your heart rate.

Try it: Splash ice-cold water on your face for 15–30 seconds, or hold an ice pack to your chest.

2. The Voo Sound (Vocal Toning)

The vagus nerve passes through your vocal cords. Vibration stimulates it.

Try it: Take a deep breath and let out a low, rumbling "Voooooo" sound. Make it loud. The vibration in your chest is what signals safety to the body.

3. Gargling

Vigorous gargling activates the muscles in the back of the throat, which stimulates the vagus nerve.

Try it: Gargle water loudly for 30 seconds, twice a day. It sounds silly, but it tones your nervous system

4. The Physiological Sigh

This is the fastest way to offload carbon dioxide and reduce stress in real-time.

Try it: Inhale deeply through your nose. Then, take a second, shorter inhale on top of it (to pop open the air sacs in the lungs). Then, exhale slowly through your mouth.

Grounded Heart Story: The Bedtime Surge

I used to think "dysregulation" was something you could power through with willpower.

Then I started noticing the moment my body would cross the line.

For me, it often shows up at bedtime—when everyone's tired, the requests keep coming, and I'm trying to hold the line on boundaries without turning into a drill sergeant. One night, my child pushed back on something simple—tone, eye-roll, the whole package—and I felt my nervous system do what it always does when it senses disrespect: it surged.

My voice got louder before I consciously chose it. My thoughts narrowed. My body felt hot. It was like I could watch the window closing from the inside.

That's what it means to be outside the Window of Tolerance. It's not that you "don't know what to do." It's that your system can't access what you know.

So I did the smallest thing that actually makes a difference: I grounded first.

I stepped back. I exhaled longer than I inhaled—twice. I felt my feet. I softened my jaw. I let the surge move through without feeding it.

Grounding is just the beginning.

Once your nervous system can return to safety, a new question naturally emerges: why do certain moments pull you out of it so fast? That's where the next step begins— learning what your triggers are really trying to tell you.

THE RIPPLE EFFECT

When you ground your nervous system, everything changes:

Your children feel safer →
They have fewer meltdowns, sleep better, cooperate more

You respond instead of react →
You parent from wisdom, not fear

Your relationship deepens
→ Your kids trust you to handle their big emotions

You stop living in survival mode →
You actually enjoy parenting again

- Your nervous system drives your parenting reactions—not your values or intentions.

- A regulated parent creates a regulated child. Safety starts with your state, not your strategy.

- Grounding is the foundation: you cannot access empathy, patience, or clarity while dysregulated.

Try This in 60 Seconds: *The 3-Breath Reset*

Notice where you feel tension. Exhale slowly (6–8 counts). Repeat twice. Name your state: "I'm in yellow" or "This is red." Ground before you respond.

One Script to Steal

"I need a minute. I'm going to step away so I can come back calm."

If This Feels Too Intense

Go slower. Start with one grounding tool. If body awareness brings up trauma or panic, consider working with a therapist trained in nervous system regulation.

The Practice: Parent Reflection

- What are your earliest physical cues of activation? (Jaw clench, shallow breathing, tight chest, hot face?) Write them down. Catching yellow prevents red.

- This week, practice the Stoplight Check three times a day —even when calm. Ask: "What color am I right now?" The more you practice in green, the faster you'll recognize yellow and red.

- Track one trigger pattern for a week: What time of day? What behavior? What happens in your body first? Patterns reveal where your nervous system needs the most support.

If you or your child gets activated while practicing this step, return to **H.E.A.R.T.-ID**™: **Name it** • **Need it** • **Next it.**

CHAPTER 2

Reveal the Emotional Root

What Your Triggers Are Trying to Tell You

The Trigger Beneath the Trigger

Michael's daughter is eight. She's bright, creative, and strong-willed. She's also started talking back. Last week, when Michael asked her to clean her room, she said, *"You're not the boss of me."*

Michael's response was immediate and intense. He grounded her for a week, took away her tablet, and spent the rest of the evening fuming. His wife gently asked, *"Don't you think that's a bit harsh for one sassy comment?"*

He knew she was right. But he couldn't shake the feeling that his daughter's disrespect was unacceptable. That if he didn't crack down now, she'd grow up entitled and out of control.

Michael was reacting to a trigger. But the trigger wasn't really about his daughter's comment. It was about something much older, much deeper.

Triggers Are Messengers

A trigger is an emotional reaction that feels disproportionate to the present situation. It's when your response is bigger, faster, or more intense than the moment calls for.

Triggers don't only show up in your thoughts—they show up in your body first. You might feel heat rise, a tight chest, clenched jaw, a buzzing in your arms, or an urgent impulse to lecture, fix, or shut it down. Treat these sensations like an early warning system: your nervous system is signaling "threat," even if the moment isn't actually dangerous. When you notice the first body cue, pause for one slow exhale and name it. That pause creates space to reveal the root instead of reacting from it.

Common parenting triggers include:

- Disrespect or talking back
- Whining or complaining
- Not listening the first time
- Sibling fighting
- Messiness or disorganization
- Emotional outbursts or crying

When these moments happen, many parents think, "**My child is the problem. If they would just stop** (*whining/ fighting/talking back*), **I wouldn't get so upset.**"

But here's the truth:

Your child's behavior is not the root cause of your reaction. It's the activator of something unresolved inside you.

Why this matters *(brain + connection)*

Revealing the emotional root means asking: *What is this really about?* When you pause to look for the emotional root, you're doing more than "figuring it out"—you're keeping the thinking brain (prefrontal cortex) online instead of letting the threat system drive the moment. And when you attune to what your child might be feeling underneath the behavior, you engage the brain's empathy circuitry, which strengthens connection. Attachment research consistently links responsive, attuned caregiving with stronger self-regulation over time—kids build better top-down control because they've been co-regulated first.

The Four Roots of Parenting Triggers

Most parenting triggers fall into one of four categories:

1. Unmet Childhood Needs

Maybe you were expected to be quiet, compliant, and easy as a child. Your needs for attention, expression, or autonomy were ignored or punished. Now, when your child is loud, demanding, or defiant, it triggers deep resentment: I wasn't allowed to be this way. Why should they get to?

Or maybe you grew up emotionally neglected. Now, when your child needs constant reassurance or struggles with anxiety, you feel overwhelmed and resentful: No one took care of me like this. I had to figure it out on my own.

Your unmet needs don't disappear. They sit inside you, waiting to be acknowledged.

Ask yourself: *Was I allowed to be loud, messy, or needy as a child?*

2. Internalized Fear Patterns

Perhaps you grew up in a home where love was conditional —earned through performance, obedience, or achievement. You learned that your worth depended on being "good enough."

Now, when your child struggles in school, refuses to try, or doesn't excel, you panic. Your nervous system registers: If they're not good enough, I'm not good enough. I've failed.

Or maybe you grew up with chaos and instability. Now, when your home feels messy or out of control, you spiral into anxiety. Your nervous system remembers: Chaos isn't safe. I have to control everything or something bad will happen.

These fear patterns were adaptive once. They helped you survive your childhood. But now they're running your parenting—and they're creating the very disconnection and pressure you're trying to avoid.

Ask yourself: *Do I feel safer when everything is perfect or under control?*

3. Attachment Wounds

If your early attachment relationships were inconsistent, dismissive, or overwhelming, you may have developed coping mechanisms that now show up in your parenting.

Anxious attachment: You may become overly enmeshed with your child, unable to set boundaries, terrified of their anger or rejection.

Avoidant attachment: You may struggle with emotional closeness, feel uncomfortable with your child's big feelings, or withdraw when they need comfort.

Disorganized attachment: You may swing between being overly involved and completely shut down, leaving your child confused about whether you're safe.

These patterns aren't your fault. But they are your responsibility to heal—because your children are learning attachment through you.

Ask yourself: *When my child pulls away, do I panic? When they get too close, do I feel smothered?*

4. Shame and Worthiness Wounds

Deep down, many parents carry a belief: I'm not enough. Not enough patience. Not enough energy. Not enough knowledge. Not a good enough parent.

When your child's behavior confirms this belief—when you yell again, when you can't soothe them, when you "fail" in front of other parents—the shame is unbearable. So you react. You blame the child. You over-correct. You try to control the situation so you can feel like you're enough again.

But you can't control your way out of shame. You can only heal it.

Ask yourself: *Do I feel like a bad parent when my child struggles?*

Chris came to this work because his business partner threatened to quit. "*He says I'm too aggressive, that I blow up over small things,*" Chris said defensively. "*But if I don't push, nothing gets done.*"

Chris's go-to emotion was anger. Employees made mistakes? Anger. Suppliers delayed orders? Anger. His partner questioned a decision? Anger. But anger, as I explained, is often a secondary emotion—a protective mask over more vulnerable feelings like fear, hurt, or shame.

The Exploration:

I asked Chris, "When you get angry at your partner for questioning your decision, what are you feeling underneath the anger?"

He paused. "*I don't know. Pissed off?*"

"Go deeper. What does his questioning mean to you?"

Long silence. Then, quietly: "*That he doesn't trust me. That I'm failing.*"

There it was. Beneath the anger was fear—fear of failure, fear of losing control, fear of being exposed as inadequate.

The Practice:

Chris began mapping surface emotions to their underlying root needs.

When anger arose, he would ask:

- **Surface emotion**: "I'm angry."
- **Underlying feeling:** "Beneath the anger, I'm feeling _____." (*scared, hurt, embarrassed, powerless*)
- **Core need:** "What I really need right now is _____." (*reassurance, competence, control, safety*)

Example from Chris's journal:

- **Surface:** Angry at employee for missing deadline.
- **Underneath:** Scared we'll lose the client and the business will fail.
- **Core need:** Reassurance that I'm competent and things will be okay.

The Shift:

Once Chris could identify the fear beneath his anger, he had choices. Instead of yelling at the employee, he took a breath and said, "This deadline was really important to me because I'm worried about losing this client. Let's figure out how to fix this together."

The employee responded with effort and loyalty, not defensiveness.

Michael's Root

Remember Michael and his daughter's comment, "*You're not the boss of me*"? When Michael sat with his reaction, he realized something painful: as a child, he had no voice. His father was authoritarian and controlling. Any sign of defiance was met with harsh punishment. Michael learned to suppress his needs, his opinions, his selfhood.

Now, his daughter's defiance triggered two things:

1. **Envy**: She gets to have a voice. I never did.

2. **Fear**: If I don't control her, she'll become disrespectful and out of control, just like my father feared I would.

His harsh reaction wasn't about his daughter. It was about the voiceless child inside him who never got to say, "You're not the boss of me."

Once Michael understood this, everything shifted. He didn't need to punish his daughter's defiance. He needed to heal his own.

David's coach referral came from his ex-wife. *"She says I'm emotionally unavailable,"* he told me flatly. *"But I don't even know what that means. I'm just... logical."*

When I asked David how he was feeling about the divorce, he shrugged. *"It is what it is."* When I asked what emotions were present when his wife left, he looked confused. *"I don't know. Nothing?"*

David wasn't being evasive—he genuinely couldn't identify his emotions. This phenomenon, called **alexithymia** (literally "no words for feelings"), often develops when emotions are consistently invalidated or unsafe in childhood. David's father was a military officer who valued discipline and control. Feelings were "weak." So David learned to disconnect from them entirely.

The Challenge:

You can't regulate emotions you can't feel. And you can't heal what you can't name. David's emotional suppression had served him well in his career (engineering rewards logic and precision), but it had cost him his marriage—and his connection to himself.

Before David could identify emotions, he needed to reconnect with his body. We started with:

Daily "Body Scan Check-Ins": Three times a day, David would pause and notice: Where do I feel tension? Warmth? Tightness? Numbness? He'd write it down without trying to label it as an emotion yet.

This was harder than it sounds. David's initial entries: "Chest: fine. Stomach: fine. Everything: fine." But over two weeks, he began noticing subtle differences: "Chest feels heavy before work meetings. Jaw is tight when I think about my ex."

The Practice - Stage 2: Sensation-to-Emotion Bridge

Once David could identify body sensations, we connected them to emotions using a Feelings Wheel:
- **Heavy chest + tired** = *possibly sadness or grief*
- **Tight jaw + hot face** = *possibly anger or frustration*
- **Stomach knot + racing thoughts** = *possibly anxiety or fear*

David kept the Feelings Wheel on his phone and consulted it daily. Slowly, his emotional vocabulary expanded from 3 words ("fine," "stressed," "whatever") to 20+.

David began practicing "**Emotion Journaling**": writing 3 sentences each night about his emotional landscape:

- "Today I felt _____ when _____."
- "The feeling showed up in my body as _____."
- "What I needed in that moment was _____."

The Shift:

Six months in, David called me after a difficult conversation with his teenage son. "*I told him I was feeling sad that we don't talk much anymore,*" he said. "*I actually used the word 'sad.' And he opened up.*"

For the first time in decades, David wasn't just thinking. He was feeling. And that changed everything.

How to Map a Trigger

Trigger mapping is a simple but powerful tool to reveal the emotional root of your reactions.

Step 1: Name the Trigger

When you have a strong reaction to your child's behavior, write down:

- **What happened** (the specific behavior or situation)
- **How you felt** (the emotions and body sensations)
- **How you reacted** (what you said or did)

Step 2: Ask the Deeper Questions

Now go beneath the surface:

- **When have I felt this way before?** (Often, the feeling is familiar from childhood)

- **What does this behavior mean to me?** (What story are you telling yourself about it?)

- **What am I afraid will happen if I don't control/fix/stop this behavior?** (Uncover the fear)

• **What did I need as a child that I didn't get?** (Reveal the unmet need)

Step 3: Connect the Dots

Look for patterns. Do certain behaviors always trigger you? Do you react most strongly when you're tired, stressed, or feeling inadequate?

You're not trying to eliminate the trigger—you're trying to understand it. Because once you see the emotional root, you can begin to heal it.

Common Parenting Triggers And Roots

Use this as a starting point—not a diagnosis. A trigger can have more than one root. For a deeper breakdown of the specific emotions driving these reactions—such as Anger, Guilt, or Shame—see *Appendix B: Troubleshooting Your Triggers.*

Format:

Trigger → Likely Root → Core Need → Grounded Response *(one line)*

Disrespect / backtalk → fear of losing control or being dismissed → worth / respect / safety → *"I won't argue. I'm here. Try again with a respectful tone."*

Defiance / "No!" → autonomy threat (old powerlessness) → autonomy + safety → *"You can choose A or B. Either way, the boundary stays."*

Whining / repeated asking → nervous system overload + unmet connection → connection + regulation → *"I hear you. I'm staying close. First breathe, then ask again."*

Homework refusal → shame / fear of failure → competence + worth → *"This feels hard. We'll do one tiny step, then pause."*

Lying → fear of punishment or fear of disappointing you → safety + acceptance → *"Thank you for telling me. We can handle the truth and still have a boundary."*

Sibling aggression → insecurity / competition for connection → connection + safety → *"I won't let hitting happen. You both want attention—let's reset."*

Public meltdown → parent shame + fear of judgment → worth + safety → *"My job is my child, not the crowd. We're safe. We'll step outside."*

Tantrums at transitions → loss of control + nervous system shift → predictability + autonomy → *"Two-minute warning. Then we go. Do you want to walk or be carried?"*

Mess / chaos at home → overwhelm + scarcity of support → rest + order + competence → *"I'm overloaded. We're doing a 5-minute reset together."*

Screen-time battles → grief / connection substitute + boundary fear → connection + autonomy → *"Screens are done. I'm here with you. Want music or a walk?"*

Bedtime resistance → separation anxiety / nervous system unable to downshift → safety + connection + rest → *"I'm staying for two minutes. Breathe with me."*

Eating struggles → control dynamic + sensory / stress → safety + autonomy → *"You choose from these options. My job is to offer; your job is to listen to your body."*

Quick questions to find the root fast:

- **"What is this protecting?"** (fear / control)

- **"What is this hurting?"** (pain / grief)

- **"What is this asking for?"** (needs / connection)

Finding the Root in Real Time

The fastest way to learn root work is to practice it in everyday moments. Watch how the same behavior changes when you look for the fear, need, or story underneath.

Example A: Homework Meltdown

Your child is in tears over homework saying, "*I'm stupid. I can't do this.*" On the surface it looks like resistance—but the root is often shame and a fear of incompetence.

You might respond: "*This feels impossible right now, and part of you is scared you won't get it. That's such a hard feeling. Let's take one breath, and then we'll take this one step at a time.*"

Example B: Sibling Rivalry

Your younger child hits their older sibling. Root work looks past the behavior to the feeling: "*You wanted that toy so badly, and when your brother wouldn't share, you felt so frustrated and powerless that your body acted. I'm going to keep everyone safe. Then we'll figure out what to do with those big feelings and what you can do instead.*"

Emotional Release & Somatic Integration

When you name the root, you've turned on the lights. But your nervous system doesn't change because you understand—it changes when your body experiences safety in real time. That's why we add a short release practice here: not to "calm down," but to help your system complete the stress response and come back home.

When you reveal the emotional root, something important happens: you stop blaming your child for what your nervous system is carrying. That's because the nervous system doesn't just store memories as thoughts—it stores them as state: tension, bracing, collapse, heat, tightness in the throat, pressure behind the eyes, a clenched jaw, a shallow breath.

Emotional release is not dramatic. It's simply your nervous system completing what it couldn't complete in the past: coming back to safety, letting energy move, and returning to presence.

Somatic integration means you don't just "get it" mentally —your body starts to believe it.

A simple release practice (2–5 minutes)

Use this any time you notice the sensations in your body—the temperature of your skin, the weight of your limbs, the rhythm of your heartbeat escalating. If anything feels too intense, slow down, open your eyes, look around the room, and return to breath and feet.

1. **Orient:** Turn your head slowly and name 3 neutral objects you can see. (This signals safety.)

2. **Lengthen exhale:** Inhale through the nose. Exhale longer than inhale (like a slow sigh). Repeat 3–5 times.

3. **Name sensation:** Where do you feel this in your body? (tight chest, hot face, heavy shoulders, etc.)

4. **Micro-move:** Let the body do a small natural movement: unclench jaw, roll shoulders, press feet, shake hands for 10 seconds, soften belly.

5. **Complete with contact:** Place a hand on your chest or belly and say: "I'm here. I'm safe enough right now."

This isn't about forcing yourself to calm down. It's about giving your system a path back home—so the insight you've gained becomes a new baseline, not just a new idea.

CASE STUDY — 2.3

Maya came to this work for "stress management," but when I asked how stress felt in her body, she looked blank. "*I don't know. I just know I should probably deal with it because I'm getting migraines.*"

Maya had learned to override her body's signals so completely that the only way they could get her attention was through pain. Growing up with a dismissive mother who said things like "You're fine, stop being dramatic," Maya learned to ignore her internal signals entirely.

The Practice:

We started with the "Traffic Light Check-In" because it's the most basic body awareness practice.

Three times daily, Maya would ask herself: "Am I in green (calm), yellow (activated), or red (overwhelmed)?" That's it. No analysis. Just a color.

After two weeks, she added: "Where in my body do I feel this?" (Green = loose shoulders. Yellow = tight chest. Red = pounding head.)

After a month, she added: "What might this feeling be called?" (Green = contentment. Yellow = anxiety. Red = overwhelm.)

The Breakthrough:

Six weeks in, Maya felt a migraine starting. But this time, instead of powering through, she paused and checked in. "Yellow. Tight neck. Anxious." She realized she'd been dreading a performance review all week but hadn't consciously acknowledged it.

She took a 10-minute walk, did some neck stretches, and texted her manager to reschedule. The migraine never fully developed.

"I'm starting to trust my body again," she said.

The Gift of Awareness

Revealing the emotional root doesn't instantly make triggers disappear. But it does something more important: it separates your past from your present.

When you understand that your reaction to your child's whining is actually about your own childhood need to be "easy," you stop blaming your child. You stop thinking, *"They're making me feel this way"*.

Instead, you think, *"This old wound is being activated. My child isn't doing anything wrong. I'm being given an opportunity to heal."*

And in that awareness, you create space. Space to choose a different response. Space to meet your child with compassion instead of reactivity.

The next step is learning how to give yourself what you didn't get as a child: connection to your own worth, your own voice, your own emotional truth.

Key Takeaways

- **A trigger is a signal:** your reaction is often bigger because something older got touched.

- **Root work asks:** What am I afraid of? What story am I telling? What did I need then that I still need now?

- **When you find the root, you gain choice:** you can respond from truth instead of survival.

Try This in 60 Seconds: *Root Finder*

Ask: "Is this Alarm (protection) or Ache (pain)?"
Then ask: "What is the need underneath?"

One Script to Steal

"I see something hard is happening. I'm here. We'll slow it down."

If This Feels Too Intense
Do less, not more. Use grounding first. Save deep root work for when you're resourced and supported.

The Practice: Parent Reflection

• Choose one moment this week where you felt disconnected from your child. Replay it in your mind, but this time, imagine dropping from your head into your body. What sensations arise? What might your child have been feeling beneath their behavior?

• Empathic attunement requires nervous system capacity. When you're depleted, stressed, or overwhelmed, attunement becomes nearly impossible. What are three ways you could create more regulation in your own system? (Examples: morning routine, boundaries with work, asking for support)

• Practice co-regulation: Sit with your child for 5 minutes in silence. Match their breathing pattern, then slowly deepen your own breath. Notice if their breathing shifts to match yours. This is your nervous system teaching theirs what regulation feels like.

If you or your child gets activated while practicing this step, return to **H.E.A.R.T.-ID**™: **Name it** • **Need it** • **Next it.**

Reconnect to the Self

Restoring Trust in Your Inner Voice

A Moment You Might Recognize

Danielle is the kind of parent who can handle a lot. She runs a business, keeps the house moving, and people count on her. But lately she feels strangely unsure of herself at home. One night at dinner, her son pushes his plate away and says, *"This is gross."*

Danielle feels heat rise in her chest. In a split second she hears two voices: one that wants to clamp down "Don't you talk like that", and another that feels small and helpless "Maybe I am doing this wrong".

She snaps, then immediately regrets it. A few minutes later she's apologizing, offering a different meal, and wondering how she got so far from the parent she wanted to be. Later, after the kids are in bed, she scrolls through advice and scripts, searching for the "right" answer. The more she reads, the less she trusts her own.

What she's really craving isn't another technique—it's a return to her inner steadiness. A way to hear her own voice again under pressure.

If any of that feels familiar, this chapter is about restoring the part of you that already knows—beneath the noise, beneath the pressure—what is true.

The Lost Self

Before you became a parent, you had a sense of yourself.
You knew what you liked, what you needed, what felt true
for you. And then you had children.

Suddenly, your needs didn't matter as much. Your identity
became "Mom" or "Dad." Your worth became tied to how
well your children behaved, how well you managed, how
well you performed the role of parent.

You started second-guessing yourself constantly: Am I
doing this right? Am I too strict? Too lenient? Am I
damaging my kids? What would other parents think?

You looked outside yourself for answers—to parenting
books, Instagram experts, your own parents, anyone who
seemed more confident than you. And in the process, you
lost touch with the one person who actually knows what
your children need: you.

This chapter is about reconnecting to yourself—not the self
you think you "should" be, but the self you actually are. The
one with wisdom, intuition, and inherent worth.

The Inner Critic vs. The Inner Voice

Many parents are intimately familiar with the inner critic—the harsh voice that says:

- **You're not doing enough.**
- **Other parents have it together. Why don't you?**
- **You're failing your children.**
- **You should be more patient/fun/present/organized.**

The inner critic sounds like it's trying to help you improve. But really, it's trying to protect you from the shame of not being "enough."

The problem? The inner critic is not your inner voice. It's the voice of your conditioning.

Your inner voice—your true self—sounds different. It's calm, compassionate, and grounded. It says:

- **You're doing your best.**
- **It's okay to make mistakes.**
- **You're allowed to have needs.**
- **You are enough, exactly as you are.**

Many parents have been listening to the critic for so long, they've forgotten what their true voice sounds like.

THE INNER CRITIC VS. THE INNER VOICE

Distinguishing Conditioning from Your True Self

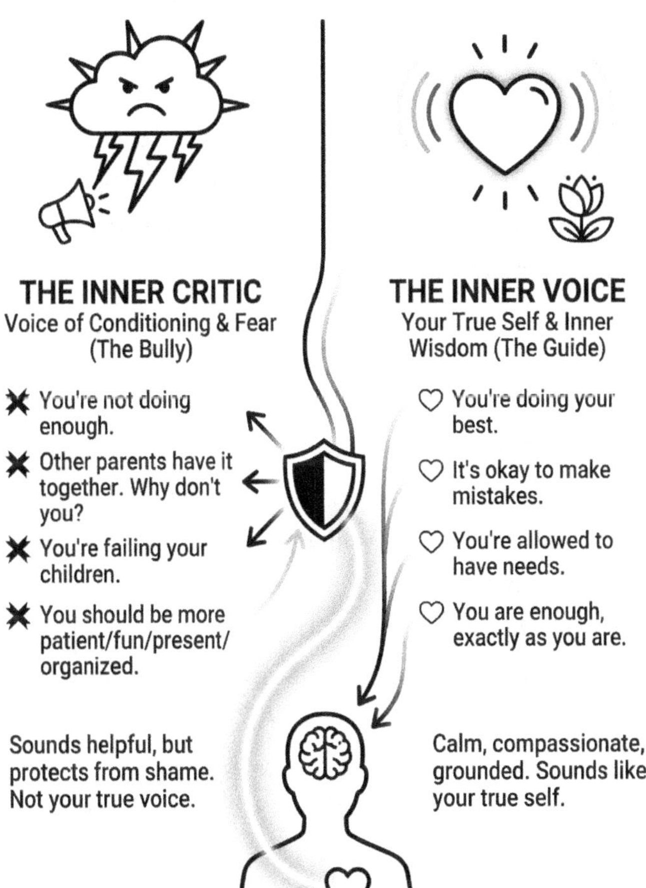

Reconnecting to the self means learning to distinguish between the two—and choosing to trust your inner wisdom instead of your inner bully.

CASE STUDY — 3.1

Alicia was outwardly successful—a partner at a prestigious law firm, respected by colleagues, admired for her precision and work ethic. But inside, she was drowning in self-criticism.

"Nothing I do is ever good enough," she said early on. *"I won a case last week, and all I could think about was the one question I stumbled on during cross-examination. I'm exhausted from trying to be perfect."*

The Root:

Alicia's parents were both academics who valued achievement above all else. A's were expected; B's were met with disappointment. Praise was rare; criticism was constant. Alicia internalized that voice. Now, decades later, she was her own harshest critic—and it was destroying her.

The Revelation:

When I asked Alicia to notice how she talked to herself after making a mistake, she paused. Then, in a small voice, she said, *"I call myself an idiot. I say things like, 'How could you be so stupid?' or 'You're going to lose everything because you're incompetent.'"*

I asked, "Would you ever talk to a child that way?"

She looked horrified. *"Of course not. That would be abusive."*

"Exactly. But you talk to yourself—the child you once were —that way every day."

That realization broke something open.

The Practice - Phase 1: Witness the Critic

Alicia began a daily practice of "**Inner Dialogue Tracking.**" Each time she noticed self-criticism, she wrote it down verbatim:

- *"You're so lazy. Everyone else is working harder than you."*
- *"You messed that up. They're going to think you're incompetent."*
- *"Why can't you just get it right?"*

Seeing these statements on paper—statements she'd been saying to herself for decades—was shocking. "I sound like my mother," she whispered.

The Practice - Phase 2: Differentiate the Voices

Next, we did Internal Family Systems (IFS®)-inspired work, identifying different "parts" of Alicia:

- **The Critic** (her internalized parental voice)
- **The Achiever** (the part trying desperately to earn love through perfection)
- **The Wounded Child** (the little girl who just wanted to be seen and loved as she was)

I asked Alicia to imagine each part as a separate person. What age was the Critic? (Her mother's age.) What age was the Wounded Child? (About 7 years old.) Could adult Alicia step in and protect that 7-year old from the Critic?

Alicia began a transformative practice: "Inner Child Dialogues." Each night, she would write a letter to her 7-year-old self from the perspective of the loving, attuned parent she wished she'd had:

"Dear Little Alicia,

I see how hard you're trying. I see you staying up late to study, trying so hard to make your parents proud. I want you to know something: You are enough exactly as you are. Your worth isn't in your grades or your accomplishments. You are lovable just because you exist.

I'm here now. I'm not going anywhere. You are safe with me.

Love,
Big Alicia"

She would read these letters aloud, hand on heart, letting the words sink into her body.

The Practice - Phase 4: Daily Self-Compassion Mantras

Alicia also adopted Dr. Kristin Neff's Self-Compassion Break — pairing the phrases with a physical gesture, hand on heart or a gentle self-hug — to embody the compassion."

The Breakthrough:

Four months into this work, Alicia made a significant error on a contract—the kind of mistake that would have historically sent her into a shame spiral for days. This time, she noticed the Critic's voice starting: "You're so stupid—"

But then, for the first time, another voice interrupted: "Hey. You made a mistake. You're human. Let's fix it."

She took a breath, placed her hand on her heart, and said aloud, "I forgive you, Alicia. You're doing your best."

She called her colleague, admitted the error, and they corrected it together. No catastrophe. No meltdown. Just... grace.

The Shame That Keeps You Disconnected

At the core of many parents' disconnection from self is shame. Shame is the belief that you are fundamentally flawed, broken, or unworthy of love. As researcher Dr. Brené Brown distinguishes it, guilt says, 'I made a mistake,' while shame says, 'I am a mistake.'

Shame shows up in parenting as:

- **Perfectionism** *(I have to get everything right or I'm a failure)*
- **People-pleasing** *(I have to make everyone happy or I'm selfish)*
- **Control** *(I have to manage everything or I'm incompetent)*
- **Comparison** *(Other parents are better than me)*
- **Hiding** *(I can't let anyone see that I'm struggling)*

Shame keeps you looking outside yourself for validation, worth, and answers. Because if you truly believed you were enough, you wouldn't need external proof.

But here's the truth: You are not broken. You are not too much or not enough. You are a human being doing hard, sacred work, and you are allowed to be imperfect.

Reconnecting to yourself means releasing the shame that tells you otherwise.

THE SHAME THAT KEEPS YOU DISCONNECTED

GUILT VS. SHAME (Dr. Brené Brown's Distinction)

Focuses on behavior. Can lead to repair.

Focuses on self. Leads to disconnection.

HOW SHAME SHOWS UP IN PARENTING

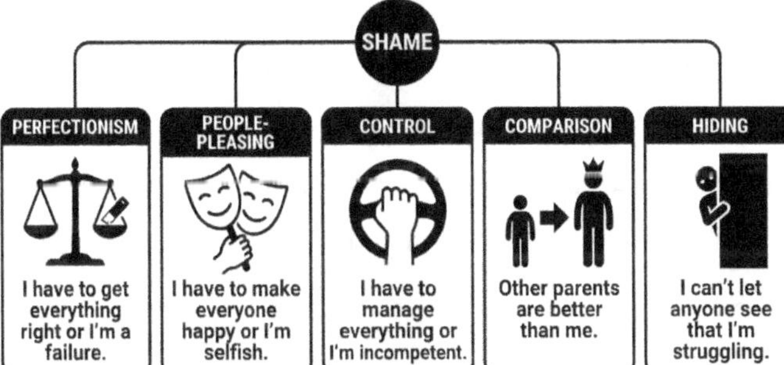

THE CONSEQUENCE: SEEKING EXTERNAL VALIDATION

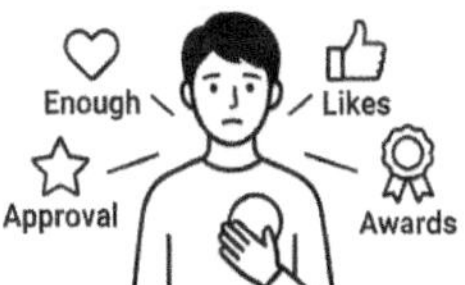

Shame keeps you looking outside yourself for validation, worth, and answers.

Because if you truly believed you were enough, you wouldn't need external proof.

THE TRUTH & RECONNECTION

But here's the truth: You are not broken. You are not too much or not enough. You are a human being doing hard, sacred work, and you are allowed to be imperfect.

Reconnecting to yourself means releasing the shame that tells you otherwise.

Nina described herself as "a recovering perfectionist in relapse." She'd redo projects five or six times, miss deadlines because nothing felt "good enough," and panic at the thought of anyone seeing her flawed work.

"I know it's irrational," she said. *"But every time I make a mistake, I feel this crushing shame, like I'm fundamentally defective."*

The Root:

Nina's mother was a perfectionist who scrutinized everything—Nina's appearance, her grades, her art. Love felt conditional: If you're perfect, I'll approve of you. If you're flawed, you're unworthy.

The Practice:

Nina began **"Imperfection Exposure coaching"**— intentionally doing things imperfectly:

• Posting a "rough draft" design on social media without editing it to death
• Sending emails with minor typos instead of re-reading them 10 times
• Cooking a new recipe without following the instructions exactly

Each time, she practiced self-compassion: "*I did something imperfectly, and I'm still worthy. I'm still lovable.*"

The Reparenting Moment:

Nina also wrote a letter to her younger self—the little girl who was trying so hard to earn her mother's love:

"*Dear Little Nina,*

You don't have to be perfect. You are enough exactly as you are—messy, creative, beautifully flawed. I love you not because of what you create, but because you exist.

Love,
Big Nina"

She read this letter aloud every morning for 30 days.

The Breakthrough:

A client asked for revisions on a logo Nina had designed. Historically, this would have triggered a shame spiral ("I'm a failure. I should have known better"). But this time, Nina paused, placed her hand on her heart, and said, "Revisions are normal. This doesn't mean I'm bad at my job. I'm doing my best."

She made the changes without spiraling. Her client was thrilled

Grounded Heart Story: Naming the Overwhelm

I grew up like a lot of us did: you keep it together. You don't make a big deal. You push through.

So when I became a dad, I assumed emotions were something to manage quietly—preferably alone.

But there was a day I didn't have the option.

I was in the car, pulled over for a minute before walking into the house, and I could feel the weight of everything I was carrying: responsibility, pressure, the sense that I needed to be strong for everyone. I kept telling myself I was "fine."

My body disagreed. My hands were tight on the steering wheel. My breathing was high. My eyes stung. And finally, instead of forcing it down, I named it—out loud:
"I feel overwhelmed."

That was it. No backstory. No justification. Just the truth.

And something in my nervous system softened. Not because the problem disappeared, but because I stopped fighting reality.

Naming the feeling didn't make me weak. It made me accurate.

That's why this work matters. When you can name what's happening in you, you stop acting it out on the people you love.

How to Practice Self-Compassion

Self-compassion is not self-indulgence or letting yourself off the hook. It's treating yourself with the same kindness you would offer a dear friend (Neff, 2011).

Notice what shifts in your body when you move from **self-criticism** to **self-compassion.** Shame often feels tight and collapsing—stomach dropping, throat closing, shoulders rounding inward. Self-compassion often brings even a small opening—one fuller breath, warmth in the chest, a softening behind the eyes. If it helps, place a hand on your heart or belly as you speak kindly to yourself. Your body will tell you when you're coming back to your true self.

Self-compassion says: "That was hard. You were triggered. You're human. What do you need right now to feel more grounded?"

Research by Dr. Kristin Neff shows that self-compassion leads to:

- **Greater emotional resilience**
- **Less anxiety and depression**
- **Better ability to repair after mistakes**
- **Stronger relationships with children**

Self-criticism, on the other hand, leads to shame, shutdown, and repeated patterns.

Three Components of Self-Compassion:

Self-Kindness (*vs. self-judgment*):
Speak to yourself with warmth and understanding,
especially when you fall short.

Common Humanity (*vs. isolation*):
Recognize that struggle is part of being human. You're not
the only parent who feels this way.

Mindfulness (*vs. over-identification*):
Notice your emotions without being consumed by them.
You can feel shame without being defined by it.

Grounded Heart Story: Meeting My Inner Child

I used to think "inner child work" sounded abstract...Then I met mine in the hallway.

One night, one of my kids got upset and slammed a door. A normal kid moment. A normal boundary moment. But my body reacted like it was 1998.

My heart jumped. My shoulders locked. I felt that old, familiar heat behind my eyes—the urge to clamp down hard, fast, now. Not because the door was dangerous... but because my nervous system associated loudness with threat.

That's when it hit me: A younger part of me was driving.

Not a "crazy" part. Not a broken part. Just a part that learned, a long time ago, that chaos equals danger—and safety comes from control. So I did something different.

I put one hand on my chest, felt the tension, and said to myself: "You're safe. I'm here."

Then I went back to my child with a grounded voice, set the boundary, and stayed connected. That's reparenting.

It's not a ceremony. It's a moment where you choose to give yourself what you didn't receive—so you don't ask your child to carry your old pain.

Reparenting Yourself

One of the most profound aspects of cycle-breaking is this:

You cannot give your children what you never received unless you give it to yourself first.

If you never learned that your emotions were okay, you have to reparent yourself by validating your own feelings now.

If you never learned that you were worthy just for existing, you have to reparent yourself by treating yourself with unconditional kindness now.

If you never felt safe, you have to reparent yourself by creating safety in your own nervous system now.

This is not selfish. This is the foundation of transformation.

Reparenting Practices

Speak to yourself the way you wish your parents had spoken to you: "You're doing your best. I'm proud of you. You are enough."

Give yourself permission to feel your emotions fully: Set aside time to journal, cry, rage, or simply sit with what you're feeling without judgment.

Meet your own needs without guilt: Rest. Play. Create. Connect. You are allowed.

Celebrate your growth: Every time you choose a different response than your parents would have, acknowledge it. You are doing hard, sacred work.

Reconnecting to Your Needs

One of the most radical acts of self-reconnection is acknowledging your needs.

Many parents believe that having needs makes them selfish. So they push through exhaustion, resentment, and depletion—and then wonder why they're so reactive with their children.

Here's the truth:

Your needs are not optional. They are the foundation of your ability to parent from a grounded heart.

When your needs are chronically unmet, you:

Resent your children for needing you

Operate from a place of depletion rather than abundance

Model for your children that self-sacrifice is love *(it's not)*

When your needs are honored, you:

Have capacity for your children's needs

Feel more patient, present, and joyful

Model for your children that self-care is an act of love *(it is)*

CASE STUDY — 3.3

Robert grew up in a household where emotions were ignored. His parents weren't abusive—they provided food, shelter, even attended his school events—but they were emotionally absent. When Robert was sad, he was told, "Shake it off." When he was scared, "Don't be a baby." When he was excited, "Calm down."

By adulthood, Robert had learned to ignore his emotional needs entirely. He excelled in his career as a paramedic—a job that rewarded emotional detachment and crisis competence. But in relationships, he struggled. Partners said he was "distant," "unavailable," "like talking to a wall."

The Presenting Issue:

Robert came to this work after his girlfriend of three years left him. *"She said I don't let her in,"* he told me, voice flat. *"But I don't even know what that means. I tell her about my day. I'm faithful. What more does she want?"*

What she wanted was emotional intimacy—something Robert had never learned to give because he'd never received it.

The Practice - Phase 1: Self-Soothing Anchors

Robert needed to learn that he could meet his own need for safety and connection. We started with "Self-Holding Practice":

When he felt the panic of potential abandonment, he would:

1. Cross his arms and give himself a gentle hug

2. Say aloud: "I'm here. I'm not leaving you. You are safe."

3. Take five slow breaths, feeling his own arms around himself

This practice activated the same neural pathways as being held by a caregiver—teaching his nervous system that he could be his own secure base.

The Practice - Phase 2: Inner Child Reassurance

Robert also began daily "Morning Affirmations to His Younger Self":

"Dear 6-year-old Robert,

Dad leaving wasn't your fault. You are lovable. You are worthy. I will never abandon you. I'm here, and I'm staying.

Love,
Adult Robert"

He'd say this while looking at a childhood photo of himself, hand on heart.

The Practice - Phase 3: Building Secure Attachment to Self

Robert practiced "Solo Dates"—intentionally spending quality time alone doing things he enjoyed (hiking, cooking, visiting museums). This helped him internalize: I can enjoy my own company. I don't need someone else to feel whole.

The Shift:

Two months later, Robert started dating someone new. She texted to cancel their Friday plans because she was tired. Historically, this would have triggered full panic ("She's losing interest. She's going to leave").

But this time, Robert paused. He placed his hand on his heart and said, "She's tired, not abandoning me. I'm okay. I've got myself."

He texted back, *"No problem! Rest up. Talk soon."* Then he made himself dinner and watched a movie he'd been wanting to see.

Common Unmet Needs for Parents:

- Rest and sleep
- Time alone to recharge
- Emotional support and validation
- Help with daily tasks
- Creative expression or hobbies
- Physical movement or exercise
- Connection with friends or partner

The Daily Need Check-In

Each day, ask yourself:
- What do I need right now?
- What is one small thing I can do to meet that need today?

It might be as simple as:
- Five minutes of silence before the kids wake up
- Asking your partner to handle bedtime tonight
- Saying "no" to one obligation
- Moving your body for 10 minutes
- Calling a friend

You don't have to meet all your needs perfectly. You just have to start acknowledging that they exist.

Practical Example: The Morning Rush

(Reconnect Before You React)

You're running late and your child is moving slowly. Your body starts to tighten. The inner critic shows up: "We are always behind. I'm failing at this."

This is a powerful moment to reconnect to yourself before you correct your child.

Take one slow exhale and ask:
What do I actually need right now? (competence? support? calm?)

Then speak from that steadier place:
"I'm noticing I'm getting stressed because we're late. Let's take this one step at a time. Are you feeling tired, or is there something you're not looking forward to today?"

This keeps you connected to yourself while inviting connection with your child—without abandoning boundaries or urgency.

Trusting Your Inner Wisdom

One of the greatest gifts of reconnecting to yourself is this: you stop looking outside yourself for answers.

You stop wondering what the parenting expert would do, what your mother would say, what the other moms think. Instead, you drop into your body, into your heart, and you ask: What feels true for me and my child right now?

Sometimes the answer is rest. Sometimes it's a boundary. Sometimes it's repair. Sometimes it's just presence.

Your inner wisdom knows. But you can only hear it when you trust yourself enough to listen.

The Mother Who Found Her Voice

Elena had always struggled with boundaries. She said "yes" to everything—playdates, school volunteering, family obligations—even when she was exhausted. When her seven-year-old daughter started having meltdowns every day after school, Elena blamed herself. I'm not doing enough. I need to be more patient, more present.

But when Elena started reconnecting to herself, she realized something: her daughter wasn't the problem. Her own depletion was. She was so overwhelmed with obligations that by the time her daughter came home, she had nothing left. Her daughter could feel it—and her meltdowns were a response to her mother's emotional unavailability.

Elena made a hard decision: she started saying "no." To the extra playdate. To the volunteer shift. To the family event.

At first, she felt terrible guilt. But slowly, something shifted. She had more energy. She could actually be present with her daughter after school. And the meltdowns decreased dramatically.

Her daughter didn't need a more perfect mother. She needed a mother who had reconnected to her own needs.

From Reconnection to Leadership

When you reconnect to yourself—when you release shame, honor your needs, and trust your inner voice—you don't just heal yourself. You transform your parenting.

Because now, instead of parenting from fear, depletion, or people-pleasing, you parent from a grounded heart. You lead your family from a place of inner stability, not external validation. You respond to your children from clarity, not reactivity. You become the calm, steady presence they need.

This is where the real transformation begins.

- **Your inner critic is often an old protector.** You can thank it without letting it drive.

- **Needs are not selfish—they're signals.** Honoring them increases your capacity to parent well.

- **Self-compassion is not "letting yourself off the hook."** It's what makes repair and change sustainable.

Try This in 60 Seconds: *The Inner Voice Reset*

Place a hand on your chest or belly. Exhale long. Say: "I'm here. I'm safe enough right now. I can take one tiny next step."

One Script to Steal (for you)

"This is hard, and I'm not alone. I can be a good parent and still have a hard moment."

If This Feels Too Intense

Slow down. Open your eyes. Orient to the room. Feel your feet. If you have trauma history or you feel flooded, consider doing this work with professional support.

The Practice: Parent Reflection

• What does your inner critic say when you're triggered? Write the exact phrases. Whose voice does it sound like?

• What are your top three unmet needs right now (rest, support, autonomy, connection, competence, worth, safety)? What is one tiny, realistic way to honor one of them this week?

• After your next parenting mistake, practice a 30-second repair with yourself first: "I'm human. I'm learning. I can repair." Notice how your tone with your child changes afterward.

If you or your child gets activated while practicing this step, return to **H.E.A.R.T.-ID**™: **Name it** • **Need it** • **Next it.**

CHAPTER 4

Lead from a Grounded Heart

Integrating Healing into Practical Parenting

When Leadership Looks Different

Carlos is tired. It's the end of a long workday and the house is loud. His daughter is bouncing off the couch, his son is arguing about homework, and the dog is barking. When a glass tips and juice spreads across the floor, Carlos feels the surge—tight throat, clenched jaw, the urge to raise his voice and take control fast.

He pauses. One breath. Longer exhale. Feet on the ground. He names it quietly: "This is overwhelm." He looks at the spill and says, calm but firm, "Stop. We clean messes together." His son rolls his eyes. Carlos feels the old impulse to punish. Instead he stays with the need underneath—competence and respect—and chooses a tiny next move: "I'm going to speak clearly. You're going to help. Then we'll reset."

Two minutes later they're wiping the floor. No lecture. No shame. Carlos didn't "win" the moment by overpowering his child—he led it by staying grounded.

That's what this chapter is about: turning healing into practical leadership in real parenting moments. When your nervous system is steadier and your roots are clearer, you can lead from connection instead of control—and your child can feel it.

The Shift from Control to Connection

For most of your parenting life, you've been taught that your job is to manage your children's behavior. To reward the good, consequence the bad, and stay in control.

But here's what happens when you lead from control:

- Your children comply out of fear, not respect
- They learn to hide their true feelings to avoid punishment
- They internalize the message: "My emotions are too much. I need to be fixed."
- The moment you're not watching, the behavior returns

Leading from a grounded heart is different. It's not about controlling your child's behavior. It's about creating safety so your child can regulate themselves.

When you lead from a grounded heart:

- Your children feel safe to express their emotions
- They learn that feelings are okay, even big ones
- They internalize the message: "I am loved even when I struggle."
- They develop internal regulation, not just external compliance

This doesn't mean permissive parenting or letting your children do whatever they want. It means parenting from connection, boundaries, and emotional safety—not fear and control.

Reality Check: Is It Defiance or Development?

So much parenting frustration comes from expecting children to have capacities their brains haven't developed yet. Before you react to "bad behavior," pause and check the biological reality:

The 3-Year-Old:

Cannot "use their words" when dysregulated. Their prefrontal cortex (the logic center) literally goes offline during big emotions.

The 5-Year-Old:

Cannot consistently remember multi-step instructions ("Go upstairs, brush your teeth, and pick out pajamas"). Their working memory isn't fully online yet.

The 7-Year-Old:

Cannot always control impulses. Their inhibitory control is still under construction. They might know the rule but lack the neural braking system to stop themselves in the heat of the moment.

The 10-Year-Old:

Cannot easily see your perspective during conflict. "Theory of Mind" (the ability to understand others' thoughts) is emerging but not solid during high-stress moments.

The Shift

When you understand what is developmentally appropriate, you stop taking behavior personally.

You stop asking, "Why are they doing this to me?" and start saying, "Oh, their brain is still under construction here. I need to lend them my regulation."

Grounded Heart Story: Raising My Voice

There was a season where I thought the solution was simple: get louder.

If my oldest daughter didn't listen the first time, my system would tighten. I'd repeat myself. My tone would sharpen. And if I'm honest, I'd raise my voice—not because I wanted to scare her, but because some part of me believed volume meant leadership.

Then I started noticing something that changed everything.

When I raised my voice, my wife would shut down. Not in a dramatic way—more like her eyes would glaze a little, her nervous system going quiet and far away. Later, through this work and conversations we had, I realized why: her childhood taught her that a man's raised voice meant danger.

And once I could see that, I couldn't unsee it. Because my daughter had the same response.

The louder I got, the less she could hear me. It wasn't defiance—it was dysregulation. It was her nervous system protecting her. And suddenly it hit me: I wasn't teaching obedience. I was teaching her body to brace.

*That was the turning point. Not "be nicer." Not "be softer." **Be safe**. Calm didn't make me weak. Calm made me effective. Calm gave them access to me.*

The Calm Communication Formula

Most parenting conflicts escalate because of how we communicate, not what we're trying to communicate.

When you're **dysregulated**, your communication sounds like: "*How many times do I have to tell you?!*" or "*Stop crying. It's not a big deal.*"

Here's the formula (in order):

---

1. **Regulate first** (10–30 seconds): Run **H.E.A.R.T.-ID**™ on YOU. Longer exhale. Feel your feet.

2. **Reflect & validate** (1 sentence): Name what you see and the feeling/need underneath. (No fixing yet.)

3. **State the boundary** (1 sentence): Clear, calm, non-negotiable.

4. **Offer a next step or choice** (1 sentence): Give a small path forward (A/B), or one doable "next."

5. **Repair when needed** (30–60 seconds later): Own your part and reconnect.

One-line template you can memorize:

"I see _____ (feeling/need). I won't let _____ (boundary). Next we'll _____ (choice/step)."

The Skill of Reflective Listening (3:1)

If you want your child to feel heard quickly, aim for roughly three reflections for every question or direction you give.

A **reflection** restates the feeling or meaning behind what your child said: *"You're mad because you wanted more time."*

A **direction** is an instruction: *"Put your shoes on."*

Try it: With consent, record a short conversation with your child. Afterward, count your reflections versus your questions and directions. Don't judge what you find — just notice.

Grounded Heart Story: The Kitchen Tornado

The first time I really tested this shift, it wasn't in a calm moment —it was right in the middle of a real one.

My daughter had made herself a snack and, as usual, the kitchen looked like a tiny tornado had rolled through—wrapper on the counter, crumbs on the floor, a dish "soaking" in the sink that would still be there tomorrow if I didn't say something.

I could feel the heat rise in my chest. The old pathway lit up: raise your voice and end this.

And then I did something that felt almost too small to matter.

I paused.

I grounded—feet on the floor, longer exhale than inhale, shoulders down.

And instead of escalating, I got clearer.

Same boundary. Same expectation. But my nervous system stayed below the line. My voice stayed steady. My face stayed open.

"Hey. Cleanup is part of the snack. I need you to reset the kitchen —now."

She did it.

Not because I "won."

Not because I intimidated her.

Because she could finally hear me.

It showed up again in the morning rush—school bag, dance bag, lunch, shoes, did you eat?

When I stayed calm and safe, she could organize and move.

When I got sharp, her system froze and we both lost time.

That moment taught me what I now say to parents all the time: your child doesn't just listen to your words.

They listen to your nervous system.

Practical Examples: *The Formula in Action*

Scenario 1: The Homework Meltdown

Your 8-year-old throws his pencil across the room and shouts, *'This is stupid! I hate math!'*

Your chest tightens. You want to lecture him about respect and responsibility.

Instead, you pause, take a breath, and ground yourself by feeling the weight of your feet pressing into the ground.

You kneel to his level and say calmly: *'I can see you're really frustrated with this homework. Math feels really hard right now.'* (Acknowledge emotion)

You wait…He nods, tears welling up.

"I get it. Sometimes when things feel hard, our bodies get really big feelings. Do you want to take a 5-minute break and have a snack, or do you want to try one more problem together first?" (Offer choice within boundary)

By staying regulated yourself, you give him the co-regulation he needs to shift from overwhelm back to engagement.

Your 5-year-old refuses to put on her coat despite being asked three times. You're already running late. You feel heat rising in your face, your jaw clenching.

Instead of yelling, you notice these sensations and silently name: 'I'm activated. I need cooperation and control.'

You take a slow breath and squat down to her eye level.

"I notice you don't want to wear your coat. And I need us to leave in 2 minutes because we have to get to school on time." (Name reality without blame)

You pause.

"Your body gets to choose: do you want to put the coat on yourself, or would you like me to help you?" (Autonomy within structure)

By offering a choice instead of a command, you honor her need for autonomy while maintaining your boundary about leaving on time.

Scenario 3: The Sibling Fight

Your two kids are screaming at each other over who gets the tablet. Your instinct is to take it away from both of them and send them to their rooms.

Instead, you ground yourself—feet on floor, deep breath— and observe for just 5 seconds.

You notice your older son's red face, your younger daughter's tears.

You step in calmly: "*Whoa. I see two people who both really want the same thing. That's hard.*" (Narrate without judgment)

You sit down between them.

"*Let's figure this out. What were each of you hoping for?*"

By not immediately solving or punishing, you create space for them to feel seen first—which is what they actually need before they can problem-solve.

As you guide your child through **H.E.A.R.T.-ID™**, make the body part of the conversation.

Children often recognize sensations before they can name emotions—tight chest, hot face, wiggly legs, heavy stomach, fists that want to clench.

Help them get curious: *"Where do you feel it?"* and *"What is your body telling you?"*

Learning to notice these cues gives them an early warning system, so they can regulate sooner—before the emotion explodes into behavior.

During a calm moment, practice with your child:

"Remember yesterday when you threw your tablet? Let's think about what your body was feeling right before that happened. Did your chest feel tight? Were your hands making fists? That's what anger can feel like in your body—and it's a signal that you need help managing something."

Teaching the language of emotion in calm moments builds access in hard moments.

Quick Recap (*keep it simple*)

Regulate first → Validate in one sentence → State the boundary → Offer a next step or choice.

(You can find this formula and other key scripts in **Appendix A** for quick access.)

Angela described her parenting as "all gas, no brakes." When her kids didn't listen, she escalated. When they pushed back, she pushed harder. "*I know I'm too intense,*" she admitted. "*But if I don't stay on top of them, everything falls apart.*"

Her eleven-year-old son had started shutting down during conflict—going silent, refusing to engage. Her eight-year-old daughter had begun lying to avoid confrontation. Angela saw these behaviors as disrespect. What she couldn't see was that her children were protecting themselves from her intensity.

The Pattern:

Angela grew up with a mother who was emotionally unpredictable—warm one moment, explosive the next. She survived by becoming hypervigilant, trying to control outcomes before they went sideways. Now, as a parent, that same vigilance had become her leadership style. When her children didn't comply immediately, her nervous system registered danger—and she escalated to regain control.

The Turning Point:

One evening, after Angela yelled at her son for ignoring her, her daughter said quietly, "*Mom, we can't hear you when you're like that. It just gets scary.*"

Scary. Her children experienced her the way she had experienced her own mother.

The Practice:

Angela began tracking the moment before she escalated—jaw tightening, voice pitching higher, a hot flush in her chest. She committed to one rule: when she felt the surge, she would pause for one breath before speaking. Just one. Not to suppress the feeling, but to buy herself a choice.

She practiced the Calm Communication Formula during low-stakes moments until it became familiar. And she learned that leadership doesn't mean never getting it wrong—it means owning it when you do.

The Shift:

One Saturday morning, her daughter spilled orange juice across the counter. Angela felt the familiar surge—loss of control, mess, chaos. Her jaw clenched. She looked at her daughter's face, already bracing for the explosion.

Angela paused. One breath. Feet on the floor.

"Accidents happen. Grab a towel and we'll clean it together."

Her daughter's whole body relaxed. *"Thanks, Mom."*

That moment wasn't about juice. It was about safety. Angela's regulated response taught her daughter something words alone never could: You can make a mistake and still be okay with me.

Emotional Co-Regulation

One of the most powerful concepts in **The Grounded Heart Method**™ is this: You cannot teach your child to regulate their emotions by staying calm and detached. You teach them by co-regulating with them.

Co-regulation means:

- Being with your child in their emotional storm, not trying to fix or stop it
- Offering your calm nervous system as an anchor
- Validating their experience while holding space for the emotion to move through

When your toddler has a meltdown about the wrong color cup, your instinct might be to say: *"Stop crying. It's just a cup. You're being ridiculous."*

This sends the message: Your feelings are wrong. You're too much.

Co-regulation sounds like: *"You really wanted the blue cup. You're so upset. It's okay. I'm here."*

You're not fixing the problem. You're not giving in to the demand. You're simply offering your presence and your calm.

And here's what happens: When your child feels safe enough to feel their feelings fully, the feelings pass. They don't get stuck. They move through.

But when feelings are shamed, suppressed, or punished, they go underground—and come back louder later.

How to Practice Co-Regulation

---

1. **Get on their level** *(physically—kneel, sit, meet their eyes)*
2. **Use a calm, warm voice** *(your tone matters more than your words)*
3. **Name the feeling** *("You're so frustrated right now")*
4. **Offer your presence** *("I'm right here with you")*
5. **Wait** *(don't rush the process—let the emotion move)*

This practice is not permissive. You're not saying "yes" to everything. You're saying "yes" to their emotional experience, even when the answer to their request is "no."

Connection-Centered Boundaries

Many parents struggle with boundaries because they believe boundaries mean being harsh, rigid, or punitive. But boundaries are not punishments. Boundaries are acts of love. They communicate:

- **"I care about you enough to keep you (and myself) safe."**
- **"I trust you can handle limits."**
- **"I'm not afraid of your big feelings."**

The key to connection-centered boundaries is this: You can hold a firm boundary while staying emotionally connected.

Example 1: Screen Time

Disconnected boundary: "That's it, you're done. I told you 10 more minutes and you didn't listen. No iPad for the rest of the week!"

Connection-centered boundary: "I know it's hard to stop when you're having fun. Screen time is over now. I'll help you turn it off, and we can pick an activity to do together."

You're holding the boundary (screen time is over) while staying connected (I'm with you in this transition).

Disconnected boundary: "I don't care who started it! Both of you, go to your rooms until you can be nice!"

Connection-centered boundary: "It sounds like you're both really upset. I'm going to keep you safe by separating you for now. When you're ready, we'll talk about what happened."

You're holding the boundary (no hurting each other) while validating their emotions (you're upset, and that's okay).

Repairing After Ruptures

Here's a truth every parent needs to hear:
- You will mess up.
- You will yell.
- You will react from your triggers.
- You will lose your patience.

The question is not *if ruptures will happen.*

The question is: *What do you do after?*

Grounded Heart Story: The Day I Snapped

I want to be clear about something: I don't teach this method because I always get it right.

I teach it because I've learned what to do after I get it wrong.

There was a day I snapped. Not violently—just sharp, impatient, cutting. One of my kids' faces changed instantly. You know that look—the one that tells you you just became scary.

My old pattern would have been to justify it. To double down. To say, "Well, if you would just listen..."

Instead, I paused. I grounded. I owned it. And I repaired.

"I'm sorry I spoke to you like that. You didn't deserve that tone. I was overwhelmed, and I took it out on you. I'm going to try again."

I didn't add a lecture. I didn't demand forgiveness. I just told the truth and came back to connection.

That moment did more to break the cycle than any "perfect" day ever could—because secure attachment isn't built by never messing up.

It's built by repair.

Repair is one of the most powerful tools in parenting.

Research shows that children who experience consistent repair after conflict develop:

- Stronger emotional resilience
- Secure attachment
- Trust that relationships can be restored
- The ability to repair their own relationships later in life

SIDEBAR: Repair is not explanation. It's restoration.

The Repair Process:

1. **Acknowledge what happened** (own your part without over-explaining)

"I yelled at you this morning, and that wasn't okay."

2. **Validate their experience** (let them know their feelings matter)

> *"I imagine that felt scary or confusing."*

3. **Take responsibility** (no "but you made me" excuses)

> *"I was feeling overwhelmed, and I didn't handle it well. That's on me, not you."*

4. **Share what you'll do differently** (demonstrate growth)

> *"Next time I feel that frustrated, I'm going to take a break before I talk to you."*

5. **Reconnect** (offer physical affection, eye contact, or a shared activity)

> *"Can I give you a hug?"*

Repair doesn't erase the rupture. But it teaches your child something powerful: People make mistakes, and love is strong enough to hold them.

The Parent Who Led Differently

Paul used to parent the way he was parented: strict rules, consequences, and very little emotional expression. When his nine-year-old son started struggling with anxiety, Paul's instinct was to toughen him up. *"You're fine. Stop worrying so much. Just go to school."*

But his son's anxiety got worse. He started having panic attacks at bedtime, refusing to go to school, clinging to Paul in desperation. Paul realized: his son didn't need to be toughened up. He needed to feel safe.

Paul started co-regulating. When his son panicked, instead of dismissing it, Paul sat with him. *"Your body feels really scared right now. I'm here. You're safe."*

He held boundaries with compassion. *"I know school feels scary. And I also know you can do hard things. I'll walk you to the door, and your teacher will be there."*

And he repaired when he got it wrong. *"I'm sorry I told you to stop worrying. Your feelings matter. I'm learning how to support you better."*

Slowly, his son's anxiety decreased. Not because Paul fixed it, but because his son finally felt safe enough to feel it—and let it move through.

Leading as the Emotional Anchor

When you lead from a Grounded Heart, you become the emotional anchor of your home.

Your children stop looking to you to fix their feelings. They start trusting that you can hold space for their feelings.

They stop needing to be perfect to earn your love. They start knowing they are loved, even in their mess.

They stop fearing their own emotions. They start learning how to feel, process, and regulate.

And you? You stop parenting from fear, control, and depletion. You start parenting from presence, trust, and love.

This is the foundation for the final transformation: ending the generational cycle.

STOP
(Fear & Control)

START
(Presence & Trust)

Children looking to you to **fix** their feelings.

Needing to be **perfect** to earn your love.

Fearing their own emotions.

Parenting from fear, control, and depletion.

Trusting that you can **hold space** for their feelings.

Knowing they are **loved**, even in their mess.

Learning how to feel, process, and regulate.

Parenting from presence, trust, and love.

- Lead with regulation, then reflection, then boundary—then offer a next step.

- Connection and boundaries can live in the same sentence.

- Repair is a skill: fast ownership rebuilds trust and teaches resilience.

Try This in 60 Seconds: *The One-Line Formula*

"I see _____ (feeling/need). I won't let _____ (boundary). Next we'll _____ (choice/step)."

One Script to Steal

"I see you're upset. I won't let hitting happen. You can stomp your feet or squeeze this pillow."

If This Feels Too Intense
Take a pause. Step away safely. Regulate first. Repair later. You don't have to solve everything mid-storm.

The Practice: Parent Reflection

• What's your own relationship with naming emotions? Can you easily identify and articulate what you're feeling, or do you default to "fine," "stressed," or "tired"? Your child will only develop the emotional vocabulary you model.

• This week, practice **H.E.A.R.T.-ID™** on yourself. When you feel activated, pause and ask: "Where is this in my body? What sensation am I feeling? What emotion might this be?" Journal your observations. This self-awareness is the foundation of teaching your child.

• Create an "Emotion Map" with your child during a calm moment. Draw a body outline and have them color where different emotions live (anger in chest/arms, fear in belly, sadness in throat, joy in heart). Put it on the fridge and reference it during emotional moments.

If you or your child gets activated while practicing this step, return to **H.E.A.R.T.-ID™: Name it • Need it • Next it.**

CHAPTER 5

Transform the Family Line

Becoming the Pattern Breaker

The Moment the Cycle Changes

Alyssa always promised herself she would do it differently. She wouldn't repeat the harsh tone, the criticism, the emotional distance she grew up with. But one afternoon, when her child refuses to get in the car, she hears her own voice come out sharp and familiar: "*Fine. Do whatever you want.*"

Her stomach drops. It's not just the words—it's the feeling behind them. She recognizes the pattern: frustration turning into withdrawal. Control turning into disconnection.

In that split second, Alyssa has a choice. Not a perfect choice—just a tiny one.

She stops. Breath. She names it: "This is fear and anger." Alarm, not wisdom. The need underneath is safety and competence. Her next move is small: "*I'm here. I got sharp. Let's reset.*" She kneels, makes eye contact, and offers one clear boundary with warmth.

The moment doesn't become magical—but it becomes different. And different moments, repeated, become a different family line.

This is what transformation really looks like—not perfection, but pattern interruption that your children can feel and carry forward.

The Inheritance You Didn't Choose

Think about your own childhood for a moment. Maybe your parents yelled. Or maybe they were emotionally distant. Maybe they were controlling, critical, or unpredictable. Maybe they did the best they could, but their best still left wounds.

You probably told yourself: I'm never going to parent like that.

And yet, here you are—yelling when you swore you wouldn't. Shutting down emotionally when your child needs you. Repeating the very patterns you promised to break.

This isn't a failure of willpower. It's the reality of generational trauma.

Important Note on *"Generational Trauma"*

By "generational trauma," I mean the nervous system patterns, relational styles, and emotional rules passed down through families—not diagnosed PTSD or clinical trauma transmission. This is about the implicit learning that happens when children absorb their parents' dysregulation, fears, and coping strategies. It's coaching language, not clinical diagnosis.

Trauma, conditioning, and survival patterns don't just affect you—they get passed down. Through your nervous system. Through your attachment style. Through the implicit messages you send about safety, worth, and love.

Your children are not just inheriting your eye color or your sense of humor. They're inheriting your unresolved pain— unless you do the work to heal it.

The good news? You have the power to be the pattern breaker. The one who stops the cycle. The one who transforms the family line.

Linda came to this work carrying the weight of three generations. *"My grandmother was beaten by her husband,"* she told me. *"My mother was verbally abused by my father. And now I'm screaming at my kids the same way my mother screamed at me. I swore I'd break this cycle, but here I am, repeating it."*

Linda's story is heartbreakingly common. Trauma doesn't just affect the person who experiences it—it ripples through families, passed down through parenting styles, nervous system patterns, and unspoken emotional rules.

The Generational Pattern:

Grandmother's generation: Physical abuse → survival mode → emotional shutdown

Mother's generation: Verbal abuse → hypervigilance → controlling parenting

Linda's generation: Inheriting both shutdown and hypervigilance → yelling to regain control when overwhelmed

Linda didn't choose to yell at her children. Her nervous system, shaped by generations of trauma, was doing what it had learned to do: mobilize aggressively when threatened.

One night, Linda's 14-year-old daughter said through tears, "*Mom, you sound just like Grandma. I'm scared of you sometimes.*"

That was Linda's breaking point. "*I don't want my kids to carry this,*" she said in our session. "*It has to stop with me.*"

The Practice - Phase 1: Mapping the Generational Patterns

Linda created a "Family Trauma Timeline"—a visual map of the patterns passed down through her lineage:

Generation → Trauma Experienced → Survival Strategy → Impact on Parenting

Grandmother → Physical abuse → Emotional shutdown, compliance → Emotionally unavailable to children

Mother → Verbal abuse, emotional neglect → Hypervigilance, control → Critical, demanding, little warmth

Linda → Inherited both patterns → Oscillates between shutdown and rage → Yelling when overwhelmed, guilt afterward

Seeing this on paper was painful—but also liberating. "*I'm not a bad mother,*" Linda realized. "*I'm carrying wounds I didn't create.*"

The Practice - Phase 2: Nervous System Regulation

Before Linda could parent differently, she needed to regulate her own nervous system. We focused on:

1. Early Warning System: Linda identified her *"rage triggers"*:

• Kids not listening after she'd repeated herself

• Messes in the house when she was already stressed

• Disrespectful tone from her teens

2. Intervention Tools: When she felt rage rising (tight chest, hot face, clenched fists), she committed to:

• **Immediate exit:** "I need a minute. I'll be right back."

• **Physiological sigh:** 3 rounds of double-inhale, long exhale

• **Grounding phrase:** "I am safe. My kids are safe. I can handle this differently."

The Practice - Phase 3: Reparenting AND Repairing

Linda couldn't undo the times she'd already yelled. But she could repair:

After a blow-up, she started practicing "**Rupture and Repair Conversations**" with her kids:

"Honey, I need to apologize. When you didn't clean your room earlier, I yelled at you in a way that wasn't okay. You didn't deserve that. I was overwhelmed, and I reacted the way my mom reacted to me when I was your age. But that's my work to do, not yours. I'm learning to handle my feelings differently. I love you, and I'm sorry."

Her daughter's response: *"Thanks, Mom. That means a lot."*

Linda also began intentionally creating new family rituals—patterns of connection and safety that her children could carry forward:

• **Weekly Family Check-Ins:** Every Sunday, each family member shared one "high" and one "low" from the week. Linda practiced listening without fixing or judging.

• **Affirmation Practice:** Before bed, Linda would tell each child: "I'm so glad you're my kid. I love you exactly as you are."

• **Modeling Self-Compassion:** When Linda made mistakes, she'd say aloud, "I messed up, and I forgive myself. I'm learning." This taught her kids that imperfection is human, not catastrophic.

Linda's son forgot to take out the trash again—historically a guaranteed explosion. Linda felt the familiar surge: heat, tightness, rage. But this time, she recognized it. She said, *"I'm feeling really frustrated right now. I need to take a breath before we talk about this."*

She stepped outside, did her breathing practice, and came back. *"Buddy, I've asked you three times to take out the trash. I'm feeling disrespected when my requests are ignored. Let's figure out a system so this doesn't keep happening."*

Her son apologized and took out the trash. No yelling. No shame. Just accountability.

INTERRUPTING THE PATTERN

WHAT YOU EXPERIENCED
Early unmet needs or stress

NERVOUS SYSTEM ADAPTATION
Protection, shutdown, or hypervigilance

AUTOMATIC PARENTING RESPONSE
Reactivity • Control • Withdrawal

CONSCIOUS INTERRUPTION
Pause • Feel • Choose differently

Awareness creates a new path forward.

What Gets Passed Down

Generational trauma shows up in families through:

Nervous System Patterns: If your parents lived in chronic stress or fear, you likely absorbed that as your baseline. You learned that the world is unsafe, that you must always be on guard. Now, even when life is calm, your nervous system is braced for danger.

Attachment Styles: If your parents were inconsistent, dismissive, or overwhelming, you developed an insecure attachment style. Now, without conscious awareness, you may recreate that same insecurity with your own children.

Beliefs About Worth: If you grew up believing love was conditional—that you had to earn it through achievement, obedience, or people-pleasing—you're likely passing that belief to your children.

Emotional Suppression: If your family didn't allow certain emotions (anger, sadness, fear), you learned to suppress them. Now, when your children express those emotions, you unconsciously shut them down.

These patterns are not your fault. But they are your responsibility to interrupt.

The Cycle-Breaking Parent

Sophia grew up in a home where anger was dangerous. Her father's rage was unpredictable and terrifying. She learned to be small, quiet, and pleasing to stay safe.

Now, as a mother, Sophia struggles when her six-year-old daughter gets angry. When her daughter yells or throws a toy, Sophia's nervous system screams danger.

Her instinct is to shut it down immediately: *"We don't yell in this house! Go to your room!"*

But Sophia is doing the work. She's learning to recognize when her reaction is about her past, not her present.

Sophia stays present. Her shoulders soften. Her daughter's breathing begins to slow. The volume drops. The eyes that were wide with anger start to settle. The small body that was bracing for danger begins to trust the connection again. This is what nervous system regulation looks like in real time—felt, not forced.

Now, when her daughter gets angry, Sophia pauses. She grounds herself. She reminds herself: My daughter's anger is not my father's rage. She is safe. I am safe. Anger is just an emotion.

Then she says to her daughter: "*You're really mad right now. It's okay to be mad. Let's take some breaths together.*"

Sophia is not passing down the message that anger is dangerous. She's teaching her daughter that all emotions are welcome, that she is safe even when she's upset.

This is cycle-breaking work.

Ikeem and Maria came to couples coaching because they were "parenting from different planets." Ikeem's approach was strict and authoritarian—rules, consequences, "because I said so." Maria's was permissive and anxious—giving in to avoid conflict, apologizing for setting boundaries.

Both were repeating what they'd learned. Ikeem's father was a harsh disciplinarian; compliance was demanded, feelings were irrelevant. Maria's mother was emotionally fragile; Maria learned early to be the peacekeeper, suppressing her needs to keep everyone calm.

Now, as parents, their unhealed patterns were colliding— and their twins were caught in the middle.

The Conflict: When their son threw a tantrum at the grocery store, Ikeem wanted to "teach him a lesson" with a firm consequence. Maria wanted to soothe and give in "just this once." They argued in the car all the way home. Their son, sensing the tension, acted out more.

The Discovery:

I asked Ikeem: *"What did you need when you had big feelings as a child?"*

He paused. *"I don't know. I wasn't allowed to have big feelings."*

I asked Maria: "*What did you need when you were overwhelmed as a child?*"

She teared up. "*I needed someone to tell me it was okay to have needs. That I wasn't a burden.*"

The Practice - Phase 1: Individual Healing

Before they could co-parent effectively, each needed to do their own reparenting work:

Ikeem practiced noticing when his "authoritarian voice" kicked in and asking, "*Am I parenting my child, or am I repeating my father's pattern?*" He began using empathy statements before consequences: "*I see you're upset. It's okay to feel that. And we still need to leave the store now.*"

Maria practiced setting boundaries without apologizing: "*I know you want another cookie, and the answer is no.*" She learned that boundaries are love, not cruelty.

The Practice - Phase 2: Co-Regulation

Ikeem and Maria began a weekly "**Parenting Alignment Meeting**":
- **What went well this week?**
- **Where did we clash?**
- **What pattern were each of us repeating?**
- **How do we want to respond next time?**

This practice helped them parent together rather than against each other.

The Shift:

Two months later, their daughter melted down at bedtime. Historically, Ikeem would have gotten stern; Maria would have gotten anxious. But this time, they tag-teamed:

Ikeem knelt down and said, "*You're really upset. Tell me what's wrong.*" (Empathy)

Maria held the boundary: "*We hear you, and it's still bedtime. Let's read one book together.*" (Firmness with warmth)

Their daughter calmed down. Bedtime happened. No fight between the parents afterward.

The Healing That Changes Everything

When you heal your nervous system, you don't just change yourself.

You change the emotional inheritance of your entire family line.

Your children will not have to unlearn:
- That love is conditional
- That their emotions are too much
- That they have to perform to be worthy
- That the world is fundamentally unsafe

Instead, they will grow up knowing:
- They are loved exactly as they are
- Their emotions are valid and manageable
- They are inherently worthy
- Their world feels more predictable and safe because you offer steadiness and repair

Practical Example: A Cycle-Breaking Moment *(Full Method in Real Life)*

Jake, age 8, typically had explosive tantrums when told "no." His mom began using the full method in the moment: she honored his disappointment ("You really wanted that, and hearing no feels terrible"), attuned to the need underneath ("You wanted choice and control today"), reflected what she saw ("Your whole body is saying NO right now"), helped him identify the emotion ("This feels like disappointment mixed with anger—do you feel it in your chest?"), and stayed connected ("I'm right here. We're getting through this together").

Over the following weeks, Jake began recovering faster and started naming frustration before he escalated—because connection replaced power struggles, and his nervous system learned a new pattern.

The point isn't that Jake stopped having big feelings—it's that the body learned a new pathway. A meltdown that used to escalate into shouting and shutdown now moved through: tension rose, a pause happened, breathing returned, and connection stayed intact. That's how patterns change over time—one regulated moment at a time, until "calm after hard" becomes familiar.

This is legacy-level transformation.

While we focus on breaking dysfunctional patterns, it is equally important to honor the gifts in your family line. We don't want to throw the baby out with the bathwater. Use this sorting method to consciously choose your inheritance.

Create three columns in your journal:

Column 1: RELEASE

List the patterns, beliefs, or behaviors that no longer serve you or your children.

Examples: Criticism as a love language, emotional suppression ("don't cry"), scarcity mindset, or control through fear.

Column 2: PRESERVE

List the strengths and wisdom you want to intentionally pass forward.

Examples: Strong work ethic, loyalty, resilience, cultural traditions, a sense of humor, or specific values like honesty and generosity.

Column 3: TRANSFORM

List the elements that have both a gift and a shadow. Your goal is to keep the gift but release the shadow.

Examples:

• Strength (gift) without Rigidity (shadow).

• High Standards (gift) without Perfectionism (shadow).

• Care for Others (gift) without Self-Abandonment (shadow).

Action:

For one week, carry these three columns with you — not just on paper, but in your awareness.

When you catch yourself expressing a **Preserve** trait, name it out loud to your children: "*This comes from your grandmother. This is part of our family.*" Let them know what's worth keeping.

When you notice a **Release** trait showing up — the sharp tone, the perfectionism, the shutdown — pause. Place a hand on your chest if it helps, and say quietly to yourself: "*This ends with me.*" Not with shame. With intention.

When you spot a **Transform** trait in action, get curious: "*Which part of this is the gift, and which part is the shadow?*" You don't have to fix it in the moment. Just see it clearly.

Awareness practiced daily becomes the foundation of change

Denise grew up in a family where hard things were never discussed. Her father's alcoholism? Never mentioned. Her brother's suicide attempt? Swept under the rug. The family rule was clear: We don't talk about it.

Denise carried that rule into her own parenting. When her marriage fell apart, she told her kids, "*Everything's fine.*" When she struggled with depression, she hid it. When her son got into drugs, she minimized it.

Now, her adult children barely spoke to her. "*They say I was emotionally unavailable,*" Denise said. "*But I was just trying to protect them.*"

The Realization: "*Silence isn't protection,*" I told her gently. "*It's isolation.*"

The Practice:

Denise decided to break the silence. She wrote letters to each of her three children:

"*I'm sorry I didn't talk to you about the hard things. I thought I was protecting you, but I see now that I was just repeating what my parents did—pretending everything was fine when it wasn't. I want to do better. If you're willing, I'd like to start having real conversations.*"

The Ripple Across Generations

When you heal yourself, you're not just changing your children's lives. You're changing the lives of their children, and their children's children.

Imagine: your great-great-grandchildren will grow up in a family line where emotional safety is the norm. Where worth is inherent. Where love is unconditional.

They won't even know the pain you're healing right now. They'll simply experience the freedom that your courage created.

This is the power of becoming a cycle-breaker.

Grounded Heart Story: The Vision of Normal

There's a picture in my mind I come back to when I'm tempted to rush this work.

It's not a dramatic moment. It's ordinary.

It's one of my kids laughing—fully relaxed—while the rest of the house is just... normal. No walking on eggshells. No emotional weather system to manage. Just safety.

That's the real goal.

Not "obedient kids." Not a perfectly clean house. Not a parent who never gets triggered.

A family nervous system that feels safe enough for joy to show up.

And if you're reading this thinking, "I've already messed up too much," I want you to hear me:

This work isn't about erasing the past.

It's about changing what your children will remember as normal.

That's how legacy is built—one regulated moment at a time.

The Legacy You Leave

Your children will not remember if the house was clean or if you made elaborate birthday parties.

They will remember how you made them feel.

They will remember:
• Whether you could hold space for their big emotions
• Whether you repaired after mistakes
• Whether they felt safe to be themselves around you
• Whether your presence felt calm or chaotic
• Whether they had to earn your love or knew it was unconditional

This is your legacy.

And the beautiful truth is: it's never too late to start building it. Even if you've been parenting in survival mode for years. Even if you've repeated painful patterns. Even if you've caused ruptures.

Repair is always possible. Healing is always available. Transformation is always within reach.

The moment you commit to doing your own healing work, everything begins to shift.

- Cycle-breaking is built from small repairs repeated over time—not one perfect moment.

- Your child learns safety through your steadiness, boundaries, and willingness to own your impact.

- Reparenting yourself is part of parenting your child: you can't give what you never received unless you first receive it in you.

Try This in 60 Seconds: Legacy Pause

Ask: "What did I learn about feelings in my home growing up—and what do I want to teach instead?"
Take one long exhale.

One Script to Steal

"I didn't get that right. I'm sorry. You matter to me. I'm here, and we can try again."

If This Feels Too Intense
Go slowly. Work in small doses. Consider support if old grief, trauma, or panic rises.

The Practice: *Conscious Parenting Reflection*

• Envision your relationship with your child one year from now if you fully commit to **The Grounded Heart Method**™. What's different? How do they express emotions? How do you respond? How does your nervous system feel in moments of conflict? Write this vision down and revisit it monthly.

• What's the biggest obstacle to implementing this method? Time? Your partner's resistance? Your own triggers? Your child's intensity? Name it specifically, then ask: "What's one small step I could take to address this obstacle this week?"

• Who in your life can support you in this practice? A co-parent, friend, therapist, or coach? Share this book with them and ask them to check in weekly: "How did you practice **The Grounded Heart Method**™ this week?" Accountability transforms intention into action.

You don't have to be perfect. You just have to be willing to see, to own, and to choose differently.

The Journey of a Thousand Repairs

The Invitation

The Grounded Heart Method™ is not a quick fix. It's not a strategy or a script. It's a way of being. A commitment to healing yourself so you can truly show up for your children.

It's choosing to ground your nervous system instead of reacting from survival mode.

It's revealing the emotional roots of your triggers instead of blaming your children.

It's reconnecting to your own worth instead of seeking validation externally.

It's leading from love and boundaries instead of fear and control.

It's becoming the pattern breaker who transforms the family line.

This is the work.

And it is sacred.

If you've made it to the end of this book, you understand now that parenting from a grounded heart is not about perfection. It's about presence. It's about choosing, again and again, to do your own healing work so your children can grow up feeling safe, seen, and deeply loved.

You've learned how to ground your nervous system, reveal the roots beneath your triggers, reconnect to your own worth, lead from steadiness instead of control, and begin transforming the patterns you inherited.

But understanding these things intellectually is just the beginning. The real transformation happens when you practice them—in the messy, imperfect, beautiful chaos of daily life.

Some days, you'll remember to ground yourself—feeling the solid support beneath you, pressing your feet into the floor, letting gravity anchor you before reacting. Other days, you'll yell first and repair later.

Some days, you'll co-regulate beautifully. Other days, you'll shut down or lose your patience.

This is normal. This is the journey. Healing is not linear. Growth is not perfect. You are not failing when you stumble. You're learning.

Grounded Heart Story: Practicing with My Youngest

With my youngest, I've had the gift of practicing this work earlier—more reps, more time, more chances to get it wrong and repair it.

And the difference is noticeable.

It's not that she never tests limits. She does. She's a kid. But I can feel how quickly I can return to center now. How quickly I can choose connection and leadership. How quickly I can repair if I miss it.

That's what practice buys you: not perfection—recovery.

And it's why I'm so serious about the Grounding Phase in **The Grounded Heart Method**™.

Because you can't parent "better" from a dysregulated state. But you can become a parent who comes back faster—and that changes the whole atmosphere of the home.

The Parent You're Becoming

Right now, you might not feel like the calm, grounded, emotionally available parent you want to be. You might still yell. You might still react from triggers. You might still feel like you're failing more days than you're succeeding.

But here's what I want you to know: The fact that you've read this book means you are already becoming that parent.

You are already choosing awareness over avoidance. Growth over guilt. Healing over hiding.

You are already breaking cycles. You are already doing the sacred work.

And with every breath you take to ground yourself by feeling the solid support beneath you, pressing your feet into the floor, letting gravity anchor you. With every trigger you map instead of react to. With every repair you offer. With every boundary you hold with love.

You are transforming.

Not just yourself.
Not just your children.
Your entire family line.

The Vision: *Six Months from Now*

Imagine yourself six months from now.

You don't yell as much. Not because you're suppressing your emotions, but because you've healed the wounds that made you reactive.

Your children come to you with their big feelings, not because they have to, but because they know you can hold them.

You trust yourself. Not perfectly, but deeply. You know your worth isn't tied to how well your children behave or how well you perform the role of "parent."

You lead your family from a place of inner calm. Not because life is easy, but because your nervous system has learned that you are safe, even when things are hard.

Your home has a different atmosphere. It's not free of conflict or mess or hard moments—but it's free of the constant undercurrent of threat. There's room to breathe. Room to laugh. Room to be human.

Your children are learning something profound, not from your words but from your presence: that people can be upset and still be safe. That mistakes can be repaired. That love doesn't depend on being perfect.

This is the Grounded Heart. And it is yours for the taking.

Not someday. Not when you've read enough books or figured it all out.

Now.
Today.
In this very moment.

All you have to do is choose it.

Permission to Be Imperfect

Before you close this book, I want you to hear this one more time:

You don't have to be perfect.
You don't have to get it right every time.
You don't have to fix everything today.

Progress in this work isn't measured by how calm you stay or how few mistakes you make.

It's measured by how quickly you return. How honestly you repair. How deeply you believe—despite the hard days —that you and your children are worthy of connection, safety, and love.

The journey of a thousand repairs begins with one.

You've taken the first step by reading this book.

Now take the next one.

And the next.

And watch what unfolds.

A 6-Week Grounded Heart Practice

If you want a simple way to turn insight into change, use the next six weeks as a gentle practice plan. Keep it small, repeatable, and real—progress comes from returning, not from getting it perfect.

Week 1: Ground the Nervous System
For one week, make regulation your only job. Practice a 60–90 second reset daily (and in the moment): exhale longer than you inhale, feel your feet, soften your jaw and shoulders, and let your body register safety.

Week 2: Practice H.E.A.R.T.-ID™ on Yourself First
Use the Micro-Mantra—"**Name it • Need it • Next it**"—on you just as much as on your child. Name the emotion, identify the core need (safety, connection, autonomy, worth, competence, or rest), and choose one tiny next move: regulate, validate, then decide boundary or repair.

Week 3: Reveal the Emotional Root
Choose one repeating trigger and gently trace it to its meaning. Ask: What story is my system attaching? What am I protecting? What am I longing for? Write it down. Clarity reduces shame and makes change possible.

Week 4: Reconnect to the Self

Practice self-trust and self-compassion in real moments. Replace self-attack with truthful kindness: "This is hard—and I'm learning." Notice how your tone and choices change when you feel worthy, not threatened.

Week 5: Lead from a Grounded Heart

Apply the method to communication: fewer lectures, more connection-centered boundaries. Use short scripts. Repair quickly. Aim for calm authority—clear, kind, and consistent.

Week 6: Transform the Family Line

Create a simple maintenance rhythm: one grounding practice, one weekly check-in, and one repair habit. The goal isn't perfection—it's a home where rupture is normal and repair is expected.

Take a breath. Feel your body. Notice you are safe. And begin again.

If you or your child gets activated as you integrate this, return to **H.E.A.R.T.-ID™: Name it • Need it • Next it.**

When You Need More Support

This book gives you a foundation. But for many parents, the deeper work—the work of clearing old trauma, releasing limiting beliefs, and rewiring nervous system patterns—requires more than reading alone.

If you've recognized yourself in these pages. If you've felt the weight of generational trauma. If you're tired of repeating patterns you swore you'd break. If you want to truly transform, not just understand...

You don't have to do this alone.

If you want guided support while you apply this work in real life, you have options. Some parents choose coaching or structured programs for accountability, pacing, and help customizing these tools to their family.

- Work through the root emotions (anger, sadness, fear, hurt, guilt, shame) that often fuel triggers
- Identify and loosen limiting beliefs about worth, control, and parenting
- Practice nervous system regulation patterns until they become more automatic
- Integrate new ways of responding into daily parenting and repair

Some parents choose the 12-week comprehensive program, which offers deep, sustained transformation across all five steps. Others choose the 6-week intensive program, which focuses on rapid emotional clearing and integration for parents ready to accelerate their healing.

Both options offer structure, support, and accountability to help you practice consistently and make change more sustainable.

If you're curious about working together, visit **www.GroundedHeartMethod.com** or reach out directly.

The first step is simply saying, "I'm ready."

Thank you for reading

THE GROUNDED HEART METHOD™

A Parent's Guide to Healing from Within and Raising
Emotionally Secure Children

By Justin Sokol

**For more information about the 6-week and 12-week
Please Visit:**

www.GroundedHeartMethod.com

H.E.A.R.T.-ID™ (60–90 seconds)

H — Halt & Ground: Pause. Exhale longer than inhale. Feel your feet. Soften jaw and shoulders.

E — Emotion Label: What heart-state is here (Protective / Grief / Needs)?

A — Alarm or Ache?: Is this protection (alarm) or pain (ache)?

R — Root + Need: What is the fear / story / unmet need underneath?

T — Tiny Next Move: Regulate → Validate → Boundary → Next Step → Repair (as needed).

Micro-Mantra: "Name it • Need it • Next it."

One-Line Calm Communication Formula:

"I see ______ (feeling / need). I won't let ______ (boundary). Next we'll ______ (choice / step)."

Fast Repair Script (30–60 seconds):

"I got overwhelmed and I ______. That wasn't okay. I'm sorry. I'm here now. Let's try again."

If You're Flooded:

Step back safely. Breathe. Feel your feet. Do the tiniest next move. Repair later.

THE 6 ROOT EMOTIONS

If you are struggling to identify why you are getting triggered, scan this list. In **The Grounded Heart Method**™ transformation programs, we look at six specific "root emotions" that often drive adult reactivity.

ANGER

- **Childhood Origin:** You learned that anger was dangerous, punishable, or "bad." You had to suppress it to be a "good kid".
- **Parenting Manifestation:** You explode over minor infractions, or conversely, you cannot tolerate your child's anger and shut it down immediately because it feels like a threat.
- **The Shift:** Anger is information. It tells you a boundary has been crossed. Your goal is to express it proportionally, not suppress it.

SADNESS

- **Childhood Origin:** Your tears were dismissed ("Don't cry," "You're fine") or ignored. You learned that sadness was weakness or a burden to others.
- **Parenting Manifestation:** You rush to "fix" your child's tears with distraction or treats because their sadness feels unbearable to you.
- **The Shift:** Sadness is a natural response to loss. Tears are not a problem to solve; they are a process to witness.

FEAR

- **Childhood Origin:** Your fears were shamed ("Don't be a baby") or you lived in an actually dangerous environment where you had to hide fear to survive.
- **Parenting Manifestation:** You are hyper-vigilant and over-protective, struggling to let your child take appropriate risks.
- **The Shift:** Acknowledge the fear without letting it drive the bus. Distinguish between "actual danger" and "old trauma".

HURT

- **Childhood Origin:** You felt rejected or abandoned, but were told you were "too sensitive".
- **Parenting Manifestation:** You take age-appropriate behavior personally. If your child prefers the other parent, you feel a deep sting of rejection.
- **The Shift:** Your child's behavior is rarely about you. It is about them.

GUILT

- **Childhood Origin:** You were made to feel responsible for your parents' feelings or well-being.
- **Parenting Manifestation:** You have difficulty setting boundaries because you feel guilty about disappointing your child. You over-function to avoid feeling like you've done something "wrong".
- **The Shift:** Differentiate between responsibility (owning your actions) and guilt (carrying the weight of others' emotions).

SHAME

- **Childhood Origin:** You were led to believe that you were bad, not just that your behavior was bad.
- **Parenting Manifestation:** Perfectionism. You hide your struggles and fear judgment from other parents. You project shame onto your child when they make mistakes.
- **The Shift:** Self-compassion. Recognizing that you are worthy of love simply because you exist, not because you are perfect.

APPENDIX C: *Tools Index*

Tool	Where	Purpose	When to Use	Time
H.E.A.R.T.-ID™	Core Tool+ Throughout	Identify state-need-next move	Hot moments (parent first)	60-90 sec
Micro-Mantra Name it-need it-next it	Core Tool +Throughout	Memory Shortcut	Anytime you're activated	10-20 sec
3-Breath Reset	Ch 1+ Quickstart	Downshift Activation	Early cue or mid-escalation	20-40 sec
5-4-3-2-1 Grounding Through Senses	Chapter 1	Interrupt spirals	Panic/spiral moments	1-2 min
Trigger Mapping	Chapter 2	Reveal Root	After Rupture Later Reflection	10-20 min
Somatic Release Practice	Chapter 2	Complete Stress Cycle	When Flooded/After Trigger	2-5 min
Self-Compassion Practice	Chapter 3	Reduce shame, increase capacity	After Mistakes	1-3 min
Needs Check-In	Chapter 3	Prevent depletion	Daily	1-3 min
Calm Communication Formula	Chapter 4	Regulated Leadership	Before Correcting	20-60 sec
Reflective Listening (3:1)	Chapter 4	Help Child Feel Heard	Conflict Moments	2-10 min
Connection-Centered Boundaries	Chapter 4	Limits without Disconnection	Transitions, conflict	Varies
Repair Process	Ch 4 + Throughout	Restore Trust After Rupture	After Yelling/Mistake	1-5 min
Legacy Pause	Chapter 5	Pattern Interruption	When old patters show up	60 sec

Now that you've explored the full **Grounded Heart Method**™ framework, you can access interactive tools and resources to support your practice. Scan the QR code below to visit the online **H.E.A.R.T.-ID**™ tool, downloadable worksheets, guided exercises, and updates."

Scan for Bonus Resources & Updates

The Grounded Heart Method™ draws from research in nervous system regulation, attachment science, trauma recovery, and self-compassion. The sources below reflect foundational works and practical resources for deeper learning.

SELF-COMPASSION

Neff, K. D. (2011). Self-compassion: The proven power of being kind to yourself. William Morrow.

Neff, K. D., & Germer, C. K. (2018). The mindful self-compassion workbook: A proven way to accept yourself, build inner strength, and thrive. Guilford Press.

ATTACHMENT AND RELATIONAL DEVELOPMENT

Ainsworth, M. D. S., Blehar, M. C., Waters, E., & Wall, S. (1978). Patterns of attachment: A psychological study of the strange situation. Lawrence Erlbaum.

Bowlby, J. (1988). A secure base: Parent-child attachment and healthy human development. Basic Books.

Siegel, D. J. (2012). The developing mind: How relationships and the brain interact to shape who we are (2nd ed.). Guilford Press.

WINDOW OF TOLERANCE AND TRAUMA RECOVERY

Ogden, P., Minton, K., & Pain, C. (2006). Trauma and the body: A sensorimotor approach to psychotherapy. W. W. Norton & Company.

van der Kolk, B. A. (2014). The body keeps the score: Brain, mind, and body in the healing of trauma. Viking.

Levine, P. A. (2010). In an unspoken voice: How the body releases trauma and restores goodness. North Atlantic Books.

POLYVAGAL THEORY AND NERVOUS SYSTEM SAFETY

Porges, S. W. (2011). The polyvagal theory: Neurophysiological foundations of emotions, attachment, communication, and self-regulation. W. W. Norton & Company.

Dana, D. (2018). The polyvagal theory in therapy: Engaging the rhythm of regulation. W. W. Norton & Company.

AFFECT LABELING AND EMOTION REGULATION

Lieberman, M. D., Eisenberger, N. I., Crockett, M. J., Tom, S. M., Pfeifer, J. H., & Way, B. M. (2007). Putting feelings into words: Affect labeling disrupts amygdala activity in response to affective stimuli. Psychological Science, 18(5), 421–428.

SHAME, VULNERABILITY, AND RELATIONAL COURAGE

Brown, B. (2012). Daring greatly: How the courage to be vulnerable transforms the way we live, love, parent, and lead. Gotham Books.

* 9 7 8 1 9 7 2 2 9 5 0 0 7 *